# THE WAY OF A WARRIOR

# THE WAY OF A
# WARRIOR

## John F. Gilbey

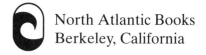
North Atlantic Books
Berkeley, California

Published by
North Atlantic Books,
P.O. Box 12327
Berkeley, California 94701

Cover art by Spain
Cover design by Paula Morrison
Typeset by Joe Safdie
Printed in the United States of America by Walsworth Publishing Co.

*The Way of a Warrior* is sponsored by the Society for the Study of Native Arts and Sciences, a nonprofit educational corporation whose goals are to develop an educational and crosscultural perspective linking various scientific, social, and artistic fields; to nurture a holistic view of arts, sciences, humanities, and healing; and to publish and distribute literature on the relationship of mind, body, and nature.

**Library of Congress Cataloging-in-Publication Data**
Gilbey, John F., 1926–
    The way of a warrior.
    "Sponsored by the Society for the Study of Native Arts and Sciences"—Verso t.p.
    1. Hand-to-hand fighting.  2. Society for the Study of Native Arts and Sciences.   II. Title.
GV1111.S69   1982   796.8'15   83–2130
ISBN 1–55643–126–0

# TABLE OF CONTENTS

# LIST OF ILLUSTRATIONS

*The author, John F. Gilbey*

# FOREWORD

*"You get what you give if you give what you
get. Don't forget it."*
—Gracie Slick

This book is about fighting and the master fighters I've known. What are
my credentials? Because I don't want to blow my own horn, let me quote what
one scholar wrote of me two decades ago.

> The author, John F. Gilbey, is one of the last of the giants. Like
> those he writes about he is a master of fighting. Heir to a textile
> fortune, he was able from an early age to begin a systematic educa-
> tion of his body. He now knows self defense like no other man alive:
> a 7 *dan* in judo and a 5 *dan* in karate, as well as the holder of master's
> certificate in Chinese boxing—the only Westener to be so accredited;
> and victor over A. Diaz, Brazilian capoeiragem champion in a
> pitched battle in 1954 which saw both the victor and the vanquished
> go to a hospital afterward. He is also a scholar, fluent in seven
> languages, and a holder of a Ph.D.

If you don't believe what you read in print—and nowadays it's smart to be
cautious—come around and perhaps I can persuade you.

On this odyssey, I've been to every continent and met superb fighters of
every race and color and sex. I've learned much from them. As a youngster, I
enjoyed the sweat, the evolving skill, and the winning. But as I grew older I
began thinking more about the role of fighting in the human sphere and
questioning whether, except as sport, fighting properly had any rightful role
in civilized society.

So, nearly 20 years after my first book, *Secret Fighting Arts of the World*
(Tuttle), I return here to the same subject—violence and how it is neutralized
and countered by effective unarmed techniques. I look at the origins and

manifestations of violent behavior in man and I compare man as a fighting entity with animals. These discussions are pointed and terse and are in no sense definitive. For the most part, though, the book is devoted—as was the first—to illuminating little-known men and women and their extraordinary methods and abilities.

My motivation for writing springs mostly from a desire to set the record straight on many forms of weaponless combat. I predicted in my first book what would happen when karate and kung fu hit the land of the big spiel. It has happened and to a worse degree than my darkest imaginings. When the dollar and any art meet, art has to lose. I give but one example. Films pretending to show ch'uan-fa (Chinese boxing)—the term "kung fu" never was used for boxing on the mainland—are celluloid products of trampolines and cameras and people out for a quick buck. Predictably, the media has shilled it for the money. If it ended there, it wouldn't be so bad but life often follows commerce and youngsters see this rot, attempt to imitate it, and get knocked down by drunk Irish welders for their pains.

I cover some of this below but let me here address an objection made to me by R. W. Smith who with Donn Draeger has been trying since the forties to put a factual and ethical platform under the Asian fighting arts. Bob tells me that my first book may have helped push this sociopathic process. He may be right but, if so, it was accidental. In my book I tried to instill discipline and I warned of the danger of commercialism. Be that as it may, this book will cause Mr. Smith no anguish.

While on the subject of the other book, because I chose not to capitalize on it, some commercial types even accused me of not existing. My friends, business associates, and especially my wife enjoyed this immensely. The implication that I don't exist is silly, but not as silly as the bird who wrote me that after reading my book he had discovered that I was his long-lost father. (A nice try, but no cigar, sir.) Nope, the sleazy merchants of vicarious violence who feel that because I don't join their nefarious trade I must not exist, should stick to their cash registers. Anyone sufficiently aware of textiles manufacture can verify my existence.

A note on my style (or as my critics would say, my lack of it). You can't please everyone. Some correspondents want rock-ribbed tightness; others carp at me for not "letting yourself go," loosening up, and even digressing when there's an interesting point to be made. Accommodating both viewpoints and realizing that style is the man, I've let my prose in this book be as varied as I am.

When Charles Dickens was getting started in the scribbling trade, he went around to get some pointers from Wilkie Collins, the famed novelist.

Collins told the young Dickens: "Make them laugh, make them cry, but above all—make them wait." In this book I don't use his advice. For a novel, go to the library. But you want to be educated, I'm trying to help you, so I can't con you with suspense. I've left out all the embroidery. The world out there is a shill much of the time; in here you deserve fact without artifice.

One other point. Taste. A fine big and sturdy word. I regard it as important. The times may be vulgar, but we needn't be. In this book I deal with violence, but nothing in it is prurient or gratuitous. The ultimate test is efficiency, and the most efficient methods and men seldom had to bloody an opponent. In fact, the greatest masters never had to fight.

This book is longer than I planned it. A lifetime seemed to seep into it in the writing. There is a risk that you may learn more about fighting than you want to know. I accept that risk. Fighting is a universal and—unhappily—a constant in this life of ours. I feel about this much as J. B. Priestly did on another subject, when he said, "No doubt there are people who have never liked the Marx Brothers . . . to them I have nothing to say." Still in all, for all red-blooded folk I think it'll be a good read.

Thus, some may find me preachy, didactic, and irreverent. Them's my friends. My enemies—and they are legion—will find me worse. But while everyone's wonderful, no one's perfect, and no one's handcuffed. So stand for what you can and when your craw gets filled use the margins of this book for grocery lists.

Finally, I must thank Dave Kaufman for his splendid illustrations. And also Terry O'Neill, former British Karate Team captain, for many kindnesses —three chapters appeared in recent years in his magazine *Fighting Arts* (Liverpool).

Thank you to John Lang, Harry Johnston, and Christine Cutting for many kindnesses.

# ICELAND: BLACK HOLES
# AND ENERGETIC FISTS

*"Nothing succeeds like failure."*
—G. K. Chesterton

In my first book I left you hanging in Iceland.

It's a fascinating place. The ancients called it Ultima Thule—the most remote place in the world. The remoteness has helped insulate its people from the torments of technology: hell, it had no towns or even villages until the nineteenth century. And today while keeping its rural values Iceland is one of only four countries with a per capita GNP over $6,500 a year. The others are all oil babies—Quatar, the United Arab Emirates, and Kuwait.

American could learn a great deal from Iceland and its friendly people. A few years ago the natives of a village in northern Iceland demanded that a planned road be moved to a new location so as not to run across a hillock used by fairies. Their petition was successful and the highway department shifted the course of the road. We Americans could stand to believe in something, if only fairies. In fact, we need the belief that comes from fairies. You say, "Hell, the Irish believed and look at them." Well, I respond that they aren't so bad. They've turned out the best writers in this century.

And some of the best fighters. Irish mercenaries fought for Louis XIV, helped gain independence for Chile, Peru, Mexico, and the U.S., were particularly active in the Boer War, and fought on both sides in our Civil War. In fact, if the Irish ever stopped fighting, the world would go pacifist from the shock of it. "Patrick, ask of your God / Does he remember their might / Or has he seen east or west / Better men in a fight?" wrote Frank O'Connor in "The Warrior". And Joseph Campbell's "A Fighting Man": "I've seen him swing an anvil / Fifty feet. / Break a bough in two, / And tear a twisted sheet . . ." But always it seems G. K. Chesterton has the total word: "For the great Gaels of

Ireland / Are the men that God made mad / For all their wars are merry / And all their songs are sad."

But back to Iceland. Five years after the incident described in my first book I spent several months in that enjoyable land trying to track down the man who had indented a steel stanchion with his fist. Now if you have to persevere on a frustrating search such as this, Iceland isn't a bad place to do it in. It had a high civilization when the natives in Britain were still painting their faces red. It has a world-esteemed literature, pivoting, interestingly, on the sagas of warriors. But what I liked most is that it is still more civilized than most major nations. It has a tiny army, almost no police, miniscule crime, no beggars or poor, and absolutely no pollution or guns. Add to this the fact that though it's a cold country it has some of the warmest women extant. So my research wasn't all that onerous.

But it was frustrating. I interviewed many physical educators and journalists about the iron-fisted man, but the consensus was always that such a creature didn't exist. Iceland has produced its own distinctive form of wrestling called *Glima* (meaning "flash"), bequeathing thousands of stalwart youths to the nation, but it has never done much with fistics. Indeed, in street fights—infrequent as they are in this pleasant land—it is considered vulgar to clench the fists.

Dr. Nils Bengt, professor emeritus of the University of Iceland, led me closest to the iron-fisted man. Nils combined the professional specialties of literature and folklore. I heard him speak one night on ancient Celtic religious impulses in the region and met him subsequently at several social functions. Later he told me of *Fotan,* a remnant of the ancient Celtic beliefs, whose members reportedly absorbed energy from the moon.

"You probably think that's lunatic," he punned. "But there are those who claim that *Fotan* still exists. There is no literature on it; if it exists, its rites are transmitted orally. But some of their priests and shamans have the ability to crush rocks and shatter stone. As a scholar I cannot confirm this. Still, rocks and stones would be minor compared with what your iron-fisted man did to a steel girder." He promised to make further inquiries. I didn't hear from him until the night before I sailed.

"Could you come over?" he asked. I could. On a perfectly purple night— the refraction of moonlight was positively eerie—I took a cab to his home at this, the eleventh hour in my research. He greeted me effusively, took me into his study and seated me in a big overstuffed chair opposite a little wasp-like man he introduced only as "John".

Nils served an excellent wine and then, *sans* ceremony, John spoke. He asked me if I'd ever heard of the black hole. I said I'd read a bit about it.

"I'm not speaking of the black hole, the energy source at the center of the sun that is gradually swallowing up solar material. I'm talking of a different black hole, an object of great theoretical importance in relativity and astrophysics. A black hole is the final stage of a dying star that is at least three times more massive than our sun. In a black hole space goes off the edge, time stops, and matter vanishes never to return. In its collapse, the star becomes so condensed that its gravitational pull will not allow anything to escape, including light. The star becomes invisible—hence its name.

"On June 30, 1908, a black hole went completely through the earth, penetrating Siberia and emerging between the Azores and Newfoundland. It was smaller than a grain of dust, weighed a million billion tons, and travelled at 25,000 miles per hour. In these holes the rules of nature are suspended. If the Earth got caught in one, we'd all perish in a flash. But some scientists say that advanced civilizations could manufacture them as casually as we build airplanes."

During John's discourse I made the appropriate courtesy sounds, though none of this was especially new to me. Then he got warmer.

"Nils has told me of your deep interest in our folklore having to do with feats of strength. I don't know personally, but in our legends our runes were able to harness a power quite beyond the natural. It was simply awesome. Some of these runes may still be among us. One of my friends who says he examined a large stone probably weighing 25 pounds when it was intact, claims that one blow reduced it to a residue resembling chalk dust! Now you can mark that off to hyperbole, especially since my friend has always obdurately refused to let me such a demonstration. When I persist in asking, he mutters something to the effect that the moon is an effective generator, but dead stars are even better. Then he catches himself and says something innocuous like, 'Our fate is in the stars . . .' I'm a scientist, and I am a born skeptic besides. But this, Mr. Gilbey, has me pondering into the late hours."

After John had left, Nils and I also pondered the thing into the late hours that night. The next day I planned to leave, to go back where I started—with just a devastating memory of the wasp-like John's implications. It was close, but close counts only in horseshoes.

A failure? Maybe. But I'd had them before and I've had some since. No sweat. After all, pardner, perfection is death. And as compensation I'd been among a vibrant people, of whom I feel as Mannheim did of the Finns: the only thing history will say of them is that there weren't enough of them!

But, fortunately for this book, for no good reason that I know, I changed my flight and the next day went swimming at a local lake. Despite the briskness of the weather, quite a few people were there swimming and lying about on the sand. After an invigorating swim I was walking in from the wet when I met her strolling into the lake, as lovely a sight as has ever pleasured me. I saw her and Reykjavik became Waikiki. Blond of course, but tall and full and curved where such things should be tall and full and curved. Young, but with eyes knowing in the he-she business, she met my inquiring eyes with a look that indicated I was a side-dish she hadn't ordered.

Nothing daunted, I sat down in the sand and watched her as she swam fluently away from the shore. Her stroke was as beautiful as the woman herself. As I watched, her form receded in the distance: she evidently intended to swim the mile or so across to the far shore. I looked away for just a moment and when I looked back across the expanse of water for her she was gone. Completely disappeared.

Did you ever notice that in a crisis your body often responds ahead of your mind? When I consciously began cogniting again I was swimming with powerful strokes and was already half-way to where I'd last seen her. What started me thinking was her reappearance up ahead and immediately I wondered if I had reacted too quickly. Perhaps she was simply breaking up the swim by some surface diving? But then I saw her arms flail wildly and she floundered and sank.

I increased the speed that had once beaten Weissmuller—Johnny was older and past his peak then—and as I entered her area I took a deep breath and dived steeply, driving myself downward. I didn't know the depth of the lake but I was going to find out. Years before I had dived fathoms deep for pearls in the Solomons but I was out of practice and with this lake I may have been out of my element. But I wasn't: I touched bottom surprisingly soon and sculled furiously. If she were stranded there I wanted water movement to push her toward the top. After what I figured was a complete circuit I came up a fathom and crisscrossed; then, as my breath began to go, shot to the top and surfaced. I looked around. Nothing. I enjoyed a few more deep breaths of ozone while watching to see if that beautiful cork would pop up. I could see a boat approaching at speed manned by three men, but no blond goddess. Down I went again for another two minutes starting with the sandy bottom and swivelling upward, spiralling always, hoping for a touch of her. But again, no, and up I came. As I surfaced and gulped air I could see the boat approaching—but no girl. A sinking dismal feeling began in the pit of my stomach. Just then, I felt this tremulous, almost lifeless, hand on the back of my shoulder, turned, and there she was, blue eyes now wild and body starting to slip under for that last fatal slide. I grabbed her with relief. And just as quickly the boat came up to us and I pushed her up into waiting hands.

Into the beach and the crowd and the lifeguard's mouth-to-mouth resuscitation. He had begun this on the boat and continued it on the beach—I almost envied him—and she came around surprisingly quickly, coughing and gagging. In a half hour we were all drinking steaming cocoa and she actually was laughing. I had my hand shook a hundred times by the group, and twice by the lifeguard, who was half-sobbing. I wondered at this until he told me he was her older brother. I could see the likeness immediately, blond, blue eyes, and an eager well-proportioned body. But as I stopped looking at her and really focused on him, a shock of recognition shot through me. Unless I was dreadfully mistaken this young man—maybe 25 or 26—was the same chap I'd seen indent a steel stanchion with his fist at the Reykjavik train station years before!

His gratitude at my saving his sister was enormous: would I accept their hospitality and have dinner with them that night? I played it coy but ended by agreeing to share their meal. One of his friends promised to return my rental car and I drove with Kathe and George—their first names, but you have no need to know their surnames—to their charming home on the outskirts of Reykjavik.

After a sumptuous repast the three of us brandied and talked late into the night. Not too late for Kathe though; after exacting a promise from me to let her show me the city the next day, that very weary girl retired.

Grateful George was a voluble conversationalist with good English acquired in the civil service. Kathe was less fluent, but with my inadequate Icelandic and the universal language of her eyes we weren't exactly Trappist. Most of the early talk predictably was on the near tragedy caused, she said, by a stomach cramp. But after she retired, George and I continued talking on a variety of subjects.

As we chatted I tried to find a peg I could hang the fighting thing on. *Fotan,* with its esoteric fistic powers—if that is what George was involved with—was so secret as to defy Iceland's greatest researchers. To get George to talk about it I'd need more than his gratitude over his sister's close scrape. I needed patience, delicacy, and luck.

But those attributes didn't swing it and as the night wore on and the pauses in our dialog lengthened, I finally realized that I had to forget diplomacy and put my cards on the table—and trust to his brotherly love. I was just on the point of pouncing, when he gave me a beautiful entree.

"John, you did a remarkable thing in saving Kathe: to swim all that distance—we were astounded at your speed—and then to search the bottom and circuit the area, finally forcing her to the surface, that was a tremendous job of swimming. I say that as a master lifeguard. Never in my life have I seen its like. Did you ever swim competitively?"

"A little. But I think the danger for Kathe motivated me and I outdid myself this time."

"I'm glad. We've been inseparable all our lives. If you hadn't been there today, for the first time in my life I would've had to learn to live alone. When I was 15, our parents died in a tragic auto accident. We've sustained each other ever since. If she had drowned today I may not have wanted to continue."

I smiled. "Happily, you don't have to face that; Kathe is very much alive."

"Yes, thanks to you. She owes her life, and I may well owe my life to you. But this is what bothers me: I have nothing with which I can repay you."

This so touched me that my better self interposed on my consciousness that it would be obscene to ask the favor that I was dying to ask. But I'm no more an angel than Mae West was and that lofty sentiment died aborning.

"George, there is something you can do for me," I began and I then recited what I had in mind. I was sure he was the man who had dented the girder at the train depot—he hesitated only a moment and then nodded—and what I was trying to do was to find what sort of energy was involved and where it originated. I told him of Nils Bengt, his mysterious friend John, who talked of black holes and stones reduced to chalk dust, and Nils' reference to *Fotan*. Did his power come from *Fotan*?

He sighed and guardedly answered.

"Yes, that was me. I hit that damned pole. Unfortunately, I can't tell you anything of *Fotan* or whether what I did had anything to do with *Fotan*. There is an enormous principle involved, a principle greater than my life or my debt to you. I'm sorry."

I sat quietly. My only chance was silence.

"What I can do," he said, breaking the silence, "is to tell you some of the mechanics involved. Would that be all right?"

"Very much. Anything you can tell me about how you defied Newtonian physics by indenting a steel girder would please me. First, did you hurt your hand?"

"No. But the hand was not the force, only the transmitter. If my hand were transformed into stone, given specific gravity and molecular density, it would not avail against steel. Wouldn't you agree?"

"Sure. So what exactly is the force your hand transmitted?"

"Force, of course, is focused power which itself depends on energy, though speed, distance, and articulation contribute. But the big thing is the energy. Energy is life. Energy is all. I have learned an esoteric method—never mind what it's called or who taught it to me or why—that lets me neutralize, you would say destroy, the very molecular structure or braiding of hard objects. Now there are many kinds of energy, most springing from maximal use of the physique. Do you know anything of Chinese boxing?"

When I nodded, he continued, "Chinese traditional boxing has some very sophisticted methods. They believe that boxing is primarily leg energy *(tu'ei-chin)* but a few experts can lightly touch a point on another's body at a certain time of day and destroy him then, or sometimes, even, after a time lag. I understand that in the old days such touches could cause death by coughing, gagging, crying, and even laughing. These esoteric methods, developed largely by solitary meditation and breathing regimes, however, needed the conjunction of method, a living opponent, time, and vital point. My method is somewhat similar in that meditation and breathing are important but the major ingredient is *borrowing*—of which I will not speak again."

He took a drink of brandy. "But I have no recourse to my physique *per se* nor to time nor the vital points of another's body. In fact, since my method works on inanimate objects quite as well as living persons, it is superbly different."

I interposed, "Has it made you a superman?"

He laughed. "No, I can't levitate as some of your spiritual smorgasborgists in America claim to do. Hell, John, you proved today you can swim rings around me—and I'm a lifeguard. No, my thing is a spillover from a deep discipline done for a higher purpose than fighting or destruction. I never fight, I can't, there wouldn't be any competition. And against guns even what I have is of no value. So fighting is at bottom foolish—as Plato said it was. That incident at the station was only an aberration by a youngster, me, who has matured a great deal since.

"Now it's getting late and I've already told you too much. But lest you get home and start wondering whether the steel of that stanchion was deficient let me cap this by demonstrating a couple of things so that you don't have to strain faith."

He got up and walked to the corner of the room where there was a croquet set, a soccer ball, and a bowling ball. He picked up the two balls and came over to my chair. Putting the bowling ball down, he held the soccer ball out.

"I'll kick this full force and it won't hit the wall," he said, and with no more ceremony he swung his foot into the black and white ball. *Into* is the correct word: unbelievably, his foot smashed into the ball, leaving him standing with the demolished remains of the ball like so many mashed potatoes hanging on his foot.

Astounded, all I could bring forth was a flippant "My God, Pele can't do that!"

George smiled and discarded the remains of the soccer ball and said,

"Now let me take this bakelite bowling ball, which is of another composition and a shape that prevents any physical force, and squeeze it flat."

And before my eyes he did just that, squeezing it flat while showing no effort! Then, holding it up with both hands in front of him, he invited me to break the flattened bakelite residue. I hopped up with alacrity and some repressed energy of my own. Focusing, I drove my right fist into the bakelite. It bent—but, combining resilience and density—didn't give.

"A good try," he said, "but you only used your body. I'll now make a bracelet of it. So saying, he tossed the mass into the air and as it descended he held his hand up. The inpenetrable stuff parted and ended by settling on his wrist!

The end, Gene Rhodes once wrote, doesn't come till along toward the last. And that was the end. I thanked him, he thanked me again for Kathe's life, and we drank another brandy. As for Kathe and me and the next day—that's none of your business. Chesterton said that the greatest thing is to be able to close your own door. I'm entitled to my measure of privacy as George was to his. So I didn't learn *how* he did his thing. I would have liked to know, of course, but it was sufficient for me to see the marvelous *what* of it. And to wonder ever since about energy and black holes and "borrowing."

# II

# GURDJIEFF'S FIZ-LES-LOO

*"It ain't nothin' till I call it."*
—Bill Klem (Major League Umpire)

I first came on the spoor of Fiz-les-loo, that "most efficient form of jujutsu," in G.I. Gurdjieff's writings.* This part mystic, part philosopher, and part charlatan claimed to have learned it from an obscure sect called the Yezidis living near Mt. Ararat in the Middle East. Gurdjieff found them a strange sect. If one of their priests drew a circle around a member, that poor soul could not of his own volition escape the circle. If forced out, he went into a cataleptic trance and came out of it only if he was put back into the circle. And from them Gurdjieff learned Fiz-les-loo. After "mastering" it, he purportedly taught a modified form of it to favored students.

Even though it whetted my appetite, I forgot about it until years later when a walleyed Walloon in Kabul, pretending to know it, called me out on the pavement. There, I promptly put his head into a basket of apricots, flushing Fiz-les-loo out of my life, I thought. But it didn't happen so. For the next day my antagonist, treating me to some concupiscent cognac, admitted he knew it not, that instead his whole arsenal of "skills" had come from a dog-eared volume on street etiquette by an American named Tegner. But he knew, he said, a man who had access to a tribe of Yezidis in Iraq who knew the secret art. The man lived in Baghdad. Would I like to meet him?

Two weeks later I was sweltering among the ziggurats of Baghdad. W. Hartman was as nice as a man who thinks Ronald Reagan is a liberal could be. He was so conservative, he thought World War II was still on. (A conservative is a man too cowardly to fight but too fat to run.) Unfortunately,

---

*I also found brief cryptic references to the art in the works of Theos Bernard, John G. Bennett, and others.

this mind-set affected everything he did. He was stingy to a fault and had the first nickel he'd ever made. Like others of this ilk he was so afraid of losing his possessions, he was quite incapable of enjoying life. Money is wasted on such as these. Tight as tree-bark, he'd been so afraid of the hotel expense when I wired him that he'd booked me into a hovel that even the bedbugs disdained.

So, owning a forest of oil wells, Hartman died his way through life. But in running fighting methods to earth, you put up with anything—even rich, stupid men.

At first he was reluctant to talk to me. When he learned I was a major shareholder in one of his companies (since the energy crisis I've divested myself of all my oil stock: it wasn't because these multi-nationals were rough —though they were that—I opted out because they were unethical), he became positively amiable.

Learning of my mission, he hesitated.

"I don't know. The Yezidis are very secretive. I have connections with one or two of them through my oil dealings. I've heard of Fiz-les-loo. Some of them still practice it, but I've never seen it."

"That may be in our favor," I said. "If they'd shown you then they might feel that you had had your favor. This way, they have a chance to give you something for the one and only time they'll ever be apt to give it to you."

He nodded. He was quick; he saw the virtue of my reasoning.

"Maybe," he mused. "Besides, they do owe me a favor. Still, even if they agree, it may cost you some money."

"No problem," I told him. "You get me a demonstration by a real expert and I'll foot the bill. And don't be niggardly." I was worried that his cheap-skate ways might jeopardize the deal.

"Okay," he said. "How much do you know about the Yezidis?"

"Damn little."

The Yezidis, he began, are a Kurdish tribal group in Iraq, Iran, and Syria, numbering now only about 50,000. Half a century ago they were three times that. In Syria people snort and call them devil worshippers, in Turkey many called them dog-collars. They all speak Kurdish and are divided into tribes, each headed by an *emir*.

"Their strange religion is a synthesis of pagan, Zoroastrian, Manichaean, Jewish, and Christian elements. They believe in Malak Ta'us, the peacock angel, God's alter ego, who filled seven huge jars with tears in 7,000 years by which the flames of hell were extinguished. So for them hell is no more.

"They are exclusive and don't intermarry with other tribes. You can't become a Yezidi—you must be born one. If a Yezidi goes abroad for over a year, he loses his wife and his religion. Only the chief priests may write.

Saturday is the day of rest and Wednesday the holy day. Each believes that he has a brother and sister in the next world. Collars of shirts, unlike other eastern shirts, are always buttoned behind.

"I understand," he continued, "that Fiz-les-loo is only practiced by the *Kharabash*, or 'blackheads', called this because of their black headgear. If true, and they permit you to see an exhibition, you must be careful. The *Kharabash* are the warrior guardians of the Yezidis and it is reputed that they rival the Gurkhas for amorality in battle."

I told him not to be concerned on that score. I was a scholar doing field research and couldn't have lived as long as I had without a strong caution bordering on cowardice.

In two days he was back by telephone, telling me that he was sending me a guide named Lupa and that he would have all the information necessary for me to consummate my mission.

"You mean they agreed!" I asked, still finding it hard to believe.

"It's all down in my directions," he said, "I don't want to talk too much about it now. Again though, I reiterate, it may be dangerous."

I told him that the turtle makes progress only when his neck is out.

"Yes," he responded primly, "but note that his ass is always covered."

That was a pretty good line, for him. I assured him of my cautionary character.

My, but he *was* a worrier, saying next: "Look, you don't *have* to do this, do you?"

"No, but I want to. And I'm not the kind of guy who when it's raining duck soup goes out with a fork."

"I see. But what it's raining may not be duck soup." He rang off then, asking me to see him when I got back.

A couple of hours later Lupa showed. He wore a burnous several sizes too big that looked like an Hawaiian mu-mu, and affected the slow, placid gait of the Bedouin. His left jaw stuck out like he had half the mumps, a sign that he was industriously chewing *qat,* that mildly narcotic leaf that is as much a social institution in those parts as Red Man chewing tobacco is in Alabama.

Lupa turned out to be a nice guy. And quite brilliant. He told me that he had brought the pertinent details and the logistic wherewithal for our trip into the mountains a month hence.

"A month?" I questioned, "I had hoped to do this business a bit more quickly."

He smiled. "You Americans are always in a hurry. There are arrangements yet to be made on the other end. But the consolation is that you will definitely be permitted to witness the Yezidi fighting rite."

He himself was acquainted with the Yezidi culture and he would be at my side to assist.

"But," he added, "if an altercation ensues, I am no longer your aide but only a simple Kurd with a family to support. After all, I know no Fiz-les-loo."

I told him not to fear, that as a diplomat I out-shone Kissinger, I said, and I was a good deal more honest than the only brother of the two who after 40 years in the U.S. still speaks with an accent.

Next he told me the price—a fairly sizable one—and I wrote him a check made out to Hartman.

Then he gave me several small manuscripts and a book from his briefcase. "These will help you while away the time before we depart," he said. Shortly after, following some cognac, he left promising to return periodically to answer any questions I might have.

Even then I didn't know whether I was being set up. True enough, he had brought the information, but there's always a problem with that, the old "whose bread I eat, his song I sing" problem. The experts they were sending me to may have been frauds who knew little of the art but were clever enough to embroider in order to fleece an outsider.

Largely on trust, however, I applied the test of the "reasonable man." And so far things looked copacetic. Having a better than average grasp of Persian and Kurdish, I plunged into the manuscripts Lupa had left. This research enabled me to absorb and sometimes edit what he would tell me in our frequent talks during the month. But I cannot vouch for its authenticity, however much it smacks of reality. I only pass it on as an inordinately interesting insight into a curious system combining combat and magic.

First off and perhaps most important, my research indicated that the art may not have originated in the area, but instead was brought in by one of the "Nine Unknown Men." The story of these august personages goes back a thousand years or more. Jacolliot, French consul at Calcutta in the late nineteenth century, stated categorically that they did indeed exist and had been responsible for scientific breakthroughs such as the liberation of energy, sterilization by radiation, and psychological warfare, all unimaginable in 1860. The serum against cholera and the plague may have come from one of these men in Madras in 1890. Talbott Mundy popularized their story in a book in 1927 but the fiction obtruded on the scientific.

Each of the nine was entrusted a book on a specific science which he was charged with continually updating. The second book was on physiology. It explained how it was possible to kill a man by touching him, death being caused by a reversal of the nerve impulse. It was said that judo was a result of leakages from this book.

I didn't turn up the book, unfortunately, but I found a reference to it in a hand-written exercise manual. I read the thing three times, and the last time it clicked. The manual, pretending to be on rudimentary school physical exercise, actually was a code version of what Yezidi initiates learned. It was too brief to be of other than general use, but the bibliography, containing only eight books craftily coded, confirmed to my own satisfaction that its citations were for the eight other books on gravitation, psychology, radiation, etc.— the province of the eight other Unknown Men. The books weren't available of course, even under their code-names, but this one was. It was on exercise, and I had a hunch that it had been introduced into this area by one of the Unknowns or a disciple. Since exercise plus secrecy plus Yezidi had to equal Fiz-les-loo, I believe that the art may have had an esoteric origin in India.

Be all this as it may, the manuscripts and Lupa provided some good material on what I was after. The adept practices only an hour a day, at 5 a.m. And only indoors. Most of the "work" does not resemble fighting. The initiate (women are forbidden to practice it) sits on the floor, his back against the walls and chants almost inaudibly the phrase "fiz-les-loo" slowly and repetitively. The chant must not be hurried. The breathing is so slow as to be almost suspended.

After a half-hour of chanting, the student ingests a special herb tea. They would not let me taste it but I got the distinct smell of coriander in the room with Gibran, the *Kharabash*, later. This is as crucial to what follows as is the chanting/ breathing regime. The tea is quaffed slowly and then the fun begins.

The heart, the theory of Fiz-les-loo is in the belief that evasion is resistance. To slip or dodge an opponent's strike is not considered kosher: it cheats your antagonist of the energy he expended and it is no test of your inner self to handle that energy. The Yezidis believe any gymnast can do what Muhammed Ali does. But the real challenge is to stand and absorb whatever your antagonist throws your way without a *visible* response.

At the end of the month the logistic arrangements being settled, Lupa and I set off on a three-day drive across acrid desert sands and through friendless mountains to the obscure village of Arbil. The trip was uneventful.

On the outskirts of Arbil, however, things began to happen. Lupa took me to a small hut and, after an elaborate greeting ritual, we were welcomed into a presentable dwelling by a man dressed all in black, the black headgear giving him away as a *Kharabash*, the Yezidi warrior caste. He introduced himself simply as Gibran. For a warrior, he appeared smallish. But you never know, and besides, "a person's a person no matter how small" (with thanks to Dr. Seuss). He was polite enough, but there was an unsettling edge to even his laughter.

After a meal and some fine wine and after Lupa had unobtrusively passed him the envelope with the moolah, we talked a while on some inconsequential matters.

Abruptly then, Gibran explained what he intended to do. And did it. He meditated for a half hour or so, then drank some tea which he didn't offer me. Then he called out sharply and a huge broth of a man entered the spacious room in which we stood. Things were moving at a rapid clip. It was obvious that we were through with the preliminaries.

Gibran put out a light arm and the behemoth shouted and clouted it with all his might. The force generated would have wiped out the suburb of a small city. But the little smile never left Gibran's face. The big boy dropped like he'd been polarized.

"That, sir, was a facial strike," Gibran observed.

I objected that, no, he had been hit in the arm.

"I did not mean my humble self—I meant him," he said, nodding at the big fellow.

Then it struck me. He was saying that the reverse energy applied by being struck on the arm had been targeted on the unfortunate's face!

Hard to believe? Well, brothers and sisters, there's more to heaven and earth—and hell—than most of us have in our theologies. Listen.

The next guy lumbering in made the first look like a midget. He towered over all of us and poor Gibran almost got lost amongst his legs. But Gibran sorted that out soon enough, and, standing in front of but considerably downhill from the fellow, offered him his stomach. The huge hulk was not pretty to start with but the countenance with which he glowered at Gibran now would have made him a contender for all-time Mr. Ugly honors. A camel kicks hard—on a pound-for-pound basis even harder than an ostrich—but the foot this guy brought up would have made a camel capitulate. He deposited this piledriver deep into Gibran's midriff. And then fell flat on his back with the kind of moan heard last along the River Styx. While Gibran stood—small, but hugely significant.

"This time, observe, sir, our friend was demolished by a—how do you say it—a groin attack," he said softly.

"But now, I must go," he continued, drawing on his robe.

I should have known better. But, amazed as I was at what had occurred, I couldn't believe that this kind of thing could happen to a man skilled in the striking arts. Gibran's antagonists had been big, true, and my medical knowledge convinced me that the thing had been on the level, but a part of me—it may have been simply arrogance, the devil that dogs all our days—wouldn't believe. And where there's no belief there's no fear—and this can get you into a passel of trouble.

"A moment, please," I said. He paused and I made my pitch.

"I am deeply appreciative of the demonstration," I started. "And thrilled by your high skill."

"It is little enough," he urged, "I am still somewhat of a novice at this in the inner councils."

I smiled. "It is difficult to conceive of anyone who would possess greater ability. I am not suggesting that there was anything charlatanical about these proceedings. Nor do I believe that your opponents were less than first rate. It is evident that they are champion fighters. But I too am a fighter. Probably much inferior to those gentlemen, to be sure, but with a different tradition and training."

"Your point, sir?" he insisted, and for the first time his voice took on a slightly testy tone.

I kept the smile that had endeared me to millions pasted on my mug and said, "Simply this. I'm curious if such a system would work against a fighting method foreign to your land. I'm fairly persuaded that it would, but, well, I guess I just want to experience it."

He looked with steely eyes into mine and said with extreme unction, "Out of the question, sir. You are our guest. One does not injure a guest. That is one way to look at it. Another is that as a guest you already have seen what most of our own people have never been permitted to see. Certainly no westerner has ever been vouchsafed the sight. Stated simply—but I hope politely—you are a guest who has been given a view of secrets accorded not even royalty."

He was saying, of course, that I was doing an Oliver Twist. Now normally, I'm a polite guy. I hold doors open for the world. But to have it implied that I was discourteous (after all, a good deal of money had changed hands), on top of gnawing disbelief, was a bit too much.

"You are right," I responded. "I ask too much. But don't you see, it is no idle curiosity. I have 30 or more years of practical fighting experience that I want to test."

"One hundred years would not avail," he said shaking his head. "Fighting, by definition, is an external art, subject, however skillful a level one attains, to the laws of physics. Regardless of the origin and present level of your skill, your ability is simply irrelevant to this case."

I was not to be put off so easily. "My skill," I said suavely, "is alas poor and low and mean. But the system behind it is none of these things. It is old and revered. And sophisticated. While it proves out scientifically, it is not limited as science is. For my system is also an internal one, based more on esoteric than on physical principles."

He started. "Esoteric, you say," he mused.

I had him then. I knew it and he knew it.

"Very well, if you insist sir. Strike me in any way your religion permits but please target it on my nose."

The nose! I had heard of a guy in England who really extends the variety of violence by claiming, *inter alia,* to be able to kill a man with his nose. Now this is no reversal of the Parisian Halitotic Attack (see my first book). No, this geezer actually uses his beezer to put the quietus on his victims. I don't know the technique he employs with this member, but it's probably a doozy. Remember the old story about the last fight you were in: how half the time you were on the bottom and the other half he was on top, or, as Artemus Ward once put it, "By a sudden and adroit movement I placed my left eye against his fist"? And how your nose kept hitting his knee? Well, our Britisher claims to be an expert on strategically placing his nose against his victim's fist where the schnoz at the moment of impact generates a double barrelled (two nostrils, you know) charge of intrinsic energy which spurts up the arm, finishing the attacker. If this is the technique, it is not one I would recommend even to masters.

But here it was in real life. And no sooner said than done. In Shanghai in 1934 while my colleagues were being drained in brothels I was being pumped full of the knowledge of the stationary strike by one ignoble gent yclept Fu Lan-chu. Fu's art consisted in being able to strike powerfully without moving his feet, or for that matter using any flexion (*e.g.,* bending the knees) of the body components. It was the idea, not the body, that did the trick. Westerners unlearned in the internal system *(nei-chia)* of Chinese boxing will howl at this —but I don't give a hoot. Fu could break one-inch *plywood* with the technique and I have no trouble doing the same.

The effect is as much in the speed with which the blow is delivered as with its incredible power. And this is how I served it up to Gibran, *sans* ceremony, flush on his nose. His head moved, of course, but he didn't fall. He just stood there with that vapid grin on his kisser.

"Are you all right?" I asked, trying to sound more considerate than I felt (after all, I don't like 'em not to fall).

"I? I am fine to be sure," he said softly, "but it is you who we are concerned with. How does your right arm feel?"

Till then I hadn't thought about the arm. It had felt good zinging out and in but I hadn't heard from it lately.

I tried to establish communication.

But there was none. No pain, no paralysis, no nothing. It was like there was no arm there at all. In Cheng-tu in 1941 an old *tien hsueh* (death touch) master had touched one of my arms and temporarily paralyzed it. But that time, even though I couldn't lift the arm, I could feel some pain in it.

But now, here, as a result of *my* punch I couldn't even feel my blasted arm. I touched it with my left hand but the neural receptor didn't even make it past some lousy synapse: I felt nothing.

"I can't locate it except with my eyes," I told him, smiling insincerely. "When I touch it, the touch isn't registered in my brain."

"But I assure you," he said, "there is no reason to worry. The charge was a minor one. You will be able to feel the arm shortly and there will be no lasting effect."

Sure enough, even as he was speaking, I felt the arm tingle, and shortly thereafter feeling surged through it.

Then I did an egregious, despicable thing. As he began to talk again—a person starting to speak is very vulnerable because of the attention his brain must give to word formation—I drove a short left hook to his groin.

Like many boxers who are natural right-handers, I had worked hard through the years to make my left superior to it. And I had succeeded. In addition I had trained assiduously in getting the maximum impact in a short compass. Short and sour was my forte.

So it was a premium shot—my best. And even now at a several years' remove from it I still think of it with admiration.

Right then, though, I put every fiber of my being into it. Contact was made. He should have died from the shock—but he didn't.

Fiz-les-loo works. I know. I had shifted all my bodyweight (220 pounds) into a blow that had carried Jim Jeffries to the world heavyweight championship (though he sometimes delivered his above the belt). As I began to retract and move back so he'd have room enough to fall, I heard a low humming sound that I couldn't place and an odor of coriander wafted by me. But that is all I remember.

I came to consciousness in a Baghdad hospital, Lupa by my side. During the week I was in the hospital, Hartman came by several times. I'll give him and his fellow conservatives this: they may not care a whit for the poor and the elderly but they will bide with those upper middle class folk they feel half-way responsible for. Look what they did for the execrable Nixon after his criminality became massive. They still suffered him.

So Hartman consoled me. But, predictably, he stopped short of picking up the hospital tab. I wouldn't have let him, of course, but I would've liked the gesture. He hadn't seen what had happened (Lord knows what Lupa told him) and wouldn't have believed it anyway. So I didn't burden him with it. He

*Gilbey's "Short and Sour"*

probably thought it was simply a case of my having been bested in combat. He really wasn't anxious to find out how. I was a loser and losers are for the dustbin. Still, he was nice to visit me during my convalescence.

I mended fast, as usual in spite of the doctors. I had two of them, western-educated, and you could tell they were puzzled. *Merck's Manual* didn't have what I had. They brought me in in massive shock as though I had been hit by a freight train. Their early prognosis was not hopeful. I learned later that the hospital had already begun to type up my death certificate.

But I recovered quickly. My rapid recovery astounded them but—even more puzzling—they could find no bruises or contusions, so were hard put to tell what had caused the injury. What they never learned, and the x-rays never divulged, was that the shock was all inside me, leaving no outward evidence of the cause.

And typically when I asked them (pretending not to know), they gave the medicine man ritual of gobbledegook. But they were insincere. Oscar Wilde in "Ballade of Reading Gaol" said that the greatest crime is inattention. I would say that insincerity is as heinous a crime. Not to be authentically yourself is to live a lie. Doctors and lawyers as a class are the biggest sinners in this regard.

At any rate I beat "Old Ned" and the "Old Rockin' Chair" in a week. Hartman didn't pay the bill. But it was paid. When the efficient little cashier told me this she gave me an envelope. Inside was this note from Gibran.

"My dear sir, my most abject apologies. In my shame, the least I can do is to use the stipend that opened the Fiz-les-loo door for you to meet your hospital expenses. I mentioned to you earlier that my skill was still that of an amateur. Hence when you attempted to surprise me my response was too great and thus nearly fatal . . . for you. I could hide my shame by quoting the words of a philosopher of this region bearing the same name as mine, "Much of your pain is self-chosen . . . even as the stone of the fruit must break, that its heart may stand in the sun, so must you know pain," but it would only disguise, not erase that shame. Therefore permit me this small token of my shame."

And that was all. But it ended well. After a week's hiatus I had walked away from hitting myself in someone else's groin.

# III

# SOME NOTIONS ON THE MARTIAL ARTS

*"Keep cool and collect."*

—Mae West

Nelson Algren once cited several eternal verities from his experience. A few I remember were:

- Never eat at a place called "Mom's"

- Never play pool with anyone named "Slim"

- Never play poker with anyone called "Doc"

- Never sleep with anyone who has worse problems than you have.

   (To which I'd add: In a public toilet, incoming traffic has the right of way.)

You get the idea. Herewith some verities I've discovered from the fighting realm.

- If you're going into a rough section of town and you have to choose between a *judoka, karateka,* or kung fu exponent to accompany you, take the *judoka.*

- If you really want to be tops on the turf, learn rigorously a short stick (like the Japanese or Filipino system) and you will have a means of self-defense superior to any unarmed one. The one problem is where in your swim trunks to stow the bloody stick when you go to the beach.

- Generally when you meet a man and he tells you about his fighting conquests, put that in the same category as the lothario who can't wait to lie to you about his last night's lay (and I refer not to billiards). Silence is man's most valuable commodity. Although I can think of several exceptions, generally, boxing mastery and glibness cannot coexist. When a garrulous dude tells you he once challenged Lew Jenkins, run from him as from the plague. You can say you're going to eat at the Borgias but you can't say you ate at the Borgias.

- There are definite diminishing returns to all human activity: boxing is no exception. Physical effort is not synonymous with directed training under a capable teacher in a competent system. Although effort is required, asceticism has produced no great boxers since Chang San-feng, about whom we know nothing reliable. Never, never sacrifice the living, shining life of a loving wife and happy children to the supposed requirements of a boxing regimen. Underline this: I have known men who traded happiness for a black belt and been miserable ever after.

- Hands are better fighting tools than feet for the simple reason that in using feet as attacking members you sacrifice their use in locomotion.

- In the street, bet on the 225-pound Irish stevedore to beat the hell out of the 125-pound 5-*dan karateka.*

- There hasn't been an honest pro wrestling match in America since 1915.

- Most Asian fighting arts imported into America, although replete with talk about ethics and self-defense, teach a sociopathic love of violence.

- This applies with equal force to judo, a so-called "sportive" endeavor. Its emphasis on early competition, awards, and winning completely negates the character-building ideal envisioned for it by its creator, Jigoro Kano.

## Status of the Martial Arts

I said in my first book in 1963 that when the Asian martial arts reached the U.S. they would be so exploited and distorted that they would resemble the original not at all. Greasing the skids they've been on ever since were the films, mainly the rash from Hong Kong. Chinese films have never achieved the artistic brilliance of their Japanese, Indian, or Western counterparts. In recent years much of the Chinese genre has profitably dealt with kung fu —and poorly, as the old French joke goes. These poor cousin attempts to outdo the Japanese *chambara* (sword saga) films have now become a fad in the west and have lowered considerably the already low level of Chinese film.

They are worse than bad—they stimulate violence and hatred. If they were simply mediocre or innocuous, that would be okay. But invariably the plots introduce Japanese, Russian, and other experts who, of course, are done in by our Chinese boxer at the end. And they always feature bloody competition between various schools. In short, the films are vehicles for violence with no redeeming value.

The boxing itself is all wrong. Anyone who has watched the free fights in Taiwan, Hong Kong, and Macau in the past 20 years knows that the celluloid doesn't resemble the real. If one tried the high kicks seen in these films in a real fight, he wouldn't last long. Low-budget flicks on boxing I saw in Taiwan and Hong Kong in the 1950's deservedly didn't make any money. The only people who watched them were pedicab drivers. My own view of their increasing popularity in the 1960's was not that more money was spent on them or that they finally got a superstar like Bruce Lee to carry them (after all, as an actor he couldn't carry Toshiro Mifune's sandals). No, they got popular because of the rise of endemic violence, particularly from the war in Vietnam, and of the need for the folks at home to have some of it, even vicarious, for themselves.

But many believe that this crud-art form was really stimulated by the boyish attractiveness of Bruce Lee, who made $9 million in three years. Donn Draeger called the Hong Kong actor "the richest guy in the graveyard." I wasn't surprised that unethical merchants commercialized this wretchedness, but I was taken aback by how the media helped ventilate it. There's even a book about the making of these celluloid cornballs, V. Glaessner's *Kung Fu, Cinema of Vengeance.* I quote one sickening excerpt: "The films are hinged on extremely skillfully shot, elongated fight sequences that opened up a whole new perspective on the term 'balletic violence' . . . The screen was alive with an ornate choreography of violence that exploited the dance-like postures of traditional Chinese martial arts." The book, thank God, ended up on the remainder lists.

Kung fu movies are to action cinema what professional wrestling is to athletics, an oversimplified lower-class entertainment without artistic seriousness. These things are plotless. They parade caricatures of characters. The bad guys in the end get what Winston Churchill liked to call "condign punishment" but not till they've escalated violence on beyond zebra. I saw a cartoon the other day showing a couple leaving a kung fu movie, and the guy is saying "Trouble is, after a half hour you're hungry for violence again!"

Our own movies have been no better. Speeded-up camera shots, trampolines and other special gimmicks, and sound effects (the sound of a fist breaking a jaw, I'm told, is a closely held secret costing $100,000) make the fighting scenes totally unrealistic. Billy Joe goes out into the street to take on a bevy of broad-based bozos. But first, he takes off his boots—which shows how little the lad knows of real fighting.

At bottom, of course, is moolah. There are big bucks in commercial martial arts. To make it in America it is not enough to be talented: you must be a salesman. There is a commercial karate studio in New York City that advertises that it doesn't take everyone who applies (only those with money). Then there is the course on self defense offered through a barbell magazine. It starts at $200, but first you have to sign a pledge that you aren't a pervert. If you keep writing in, the price progressively drops until it reaches $30 and no pledge is necessary! And oh, the lies! I heard just yesterday of a mantis boxer who could throw a soccer ball into the air and then put his fist into it. Or the fellow in Syracuse who printed up a bunch of name cards advertising his deadly wares after completing a 20-hour course in something or other. He couldn't knock the skin off a rice pudding. Called in the street once, he reached back to get his wallet so he could give his antagonist a card, and the bird used the advantage to punch him out with one right cross to the stiff lower lip.

Even qualified persons have to be careful. Skill should not forsake sanity. M. Mochizuki, the aikido master in Paris, told how a judo 3-*dan* he knew found a burglar armed with a saber in his house. The *judoka* told the burglar of his grade and his devastating power. It so frightened the burglar that he swung the saber and cut off the *judoka*'s arm.

You don't have to go to America or France to find such silliness. A so-called samurai in Kyoto issues literature which states that if all the tiles he had broken in the past 33 years were piled up they would be as high as Mt. Fuji. The implication he'd like to leave, of course, is that he can knock down Fuji. The breaking is bad enough. Tall tales of piercing power are worse. I heard of a karate expert who purportedly can explode a chicken from a distance with a concentrated *ch'i* attack. Such guys are wastes of space.

It's said that some masters with their bare hands can penetrate a human's epidermis and pull out the intestines. Shades of the so-called psychic surgery in the Phillipines and South America! Well, hear and heed, friends. It simply can't be done. If you want to prove it to yourself, toss a quarter of beef or a deer's carcass across a fence. And spear away. You and the greatest knife-hand master of all time have a lot in common: both of you will break your fingers off long before you ever penetrate the skin of the animal. People shouldn't be gulled by these glib garbagers.

One famous *karateka* claims to have beaten bulls in the ring. It's all in the definition. If you can make it broad enough to cover small, docile creatures, maybe. But if you're talking about real bulls, even the Iowa farm variety—forget it. And if it's a fighting bull like those in Spanish rings, you gotta be kidding. Sure, a good cape man can avoid them—once. But they never let the same bull fight twice: the beast learns too quickly and it would be curtains for the fighter the second time out. Add to that the fact that they don't fight these bulls barehanded. They're bled to death with pics and finally executed with a sword: certainly not by bare hands. Even Papa Hemingway with all his writing skill couldn't make the bullfight an art. If you ever hear of anyone fighting a bull barehanded, bet the bull.

There's a guy in the midwest who calls himself a 4-skull master and keeps the skulls of the four men he's killed up over his mantle. That's higher grade than a fourth black belt, I guess. Such as these are masters really of only one things, confabulation, where the hoaxer comes to believe his own hoax. I talked to a chap a while back in Austin who told me he'd had three death matches. I asked him if he'd lost any, but the poor guy didn't understand.

And how about the purported 9th degree black belt Chinese boxer in Ohio—since when did the Chinese give black belts?—who talks via ESP with his teacher in Taiwan once a week. In Hong Kong last month I saw an ad for "Super Chinese Kung-fu Troupe" one act of which was "eight blows in one second, fastest Chinese boxing in the world." And the softest: at that speed, you wouldn't even disturb Shirley Temple's curls. And then there's the immortal Li Sung of Liverpool, a merchant seaman, who, though tiny by Western standards, didn't really get warmed up until a half dozen men faced him. Once, the half dozen wore brass knuckles and so Li had to revert to the esoteric. He gestured, intoned a magical chant, and then swung into action, and it was curtains for those gents. Another time, angered at what his captain said, he swung his fist down on the captain's mahogany desk, breaking off a sizable chunk.

Such tall tales include the British master whose hands travel at 380 mph—half the speed of sound—and who claims to be able to kill a man with his nose! And there is a Chinese waiter in Manchester who, outraged because his car was ticketed, kicked the parking meter over so the top half was at right angles. Another one: a Tae KwonDo expert in Bristol jumped over eight men, smashed four 1-inch boards, and then shattered the dojo door, landing in the alley outside.

Many will believe anything. If a man is Chinese, he can do or say anything on the subject of kung fu—and be believed. In the last five years I've met 30 former mayors of Chungking, 20 of whom were taught the "secret" Yang method of t'ai-chi. Belief is a funny thing. Some Triads (Chinese secret society members) believed that a sword of peachwood would decapitate enemies when merely flourished in the air. In Nigeria not too many years ago, a witchdoctor was put to death for selling a charm to a farmer which would make him "the greatest hunter of the century" and invulnerable to bullets. Then the slap-happy witchdoctor blasted him with a shotgun to prove its efficiency. Alas, the charm didn't work.

Sadly enough, seeing is not believing. I saw a photo in a Hong Kong magazine recently which purported to show some enterprising cretin with his head on a block and a friend (?) coming down on it with a sledgehammer! Nothing is ever new. In the gay old days of pugilism there was a chap named Billy Wells who would allow his head to be pounded *through* an iron block with a sledgehammer! Which reminds me of the story of a *karateka* who carried a little satchel around giving demonstrations. He'd open it, take out a mallet, and proceed to beat his own brains out. A reporter noticed something else in the satchel and asked what it was. The demented one pulled out a bottle and said succinctly, "Aspirin."

But the two champion stories of the genre are these. A fellow robs a bank with a *nunchaku*. He gets the dough and is so surprised and exuberant that he pauses in his exit to give the tellers a free demonstration. He starts twirling the thing, gets carried away with it, and ends by conking himself on the head and going off to dreamsville. The second is a UPI story of March 30, 1975, about a 50-year old British bricklayer, Alexander Mitchell, who died after laughing non-stop for 25 minutes at a Scotsman on TV fighting his bagpipes with kung fu. His wife thanked the producers for making Alex's last minutes so happy.

Remember the young ballplayer Leo Durocher once hired? Ahead in a game, Durocher thought he'd give the kid a chance and inserted him in center field. Alas, the lad dropped the first three balls to come his way, and the score was tied. Durocher replaced him with himself. He then dropped the next two and lost the game. Afterward he growled, "You've screwed the field up so much now nobody can play it!"

Legitimate systems and teachers have trouble following these yahoos. Let me put the quietus on this part of the discussion by reciting a ditty I made up and didn't offer Nashville. It puts my feelings on the matter pretty succinctly. It's called "Let's Go Kung fuing Tonight."

I'm too meek to streak,
A rube at the tube,
But I'm ahead of the game
I'm out for fame—
Let's go kung fuing tonight.

Who's gonna stare,
Whatta we care?
Let's let down our hair
And go kung fuing tonight.

Let's jab and slice
Regardless of price;
Chop 'em pell-mell
Kick and holler like hell.

That's our dream
To hear 'em scream;
What a delight,
It's outa sight—
Let's go kung fuing tonight.


## Mysticism and the Martial Arts

Currently, America has as many satori seekers as bogus masters of the martial arts. A giant grabbag of silicone spiritualism, America has gone from yoga, through Zen and primal scream and encounter groups to the silly synthesis, Est, in two decades. Take Carlos Castaneda. For his Don Juan stories, he took Taoism, Zen, and samurai tradition, put them into a Mexican milieu, and made a mint. Almost nothing he uses is original and certainly nothing is Mexican. His mystery man ("I'm not a master, I'm a warrior") serves up Asian lines like chow mein ("The idea of death is the only thing that tempers our spirit.") Don Juan appropriates the *tan-t'ien* (navel psychic center) and other Asian artifacts. His idea that the warrior is the only one who handles the world well is a samurai/Zen derivation that is itself, dubious at best. But it makes great reading. The books met the market beautifully. The first arrived touting drugs as the means of satori at the time of their first wholesale use here. Then when the reaction came, Don Juan tells us that the mystic experience can also be achieved by meditation. Finally, in the later books he rejects drugs just when our culture found that it could live without them.

Zen has been mixed up in the warrior business for a long time, but it has been going downhill since it got organized and became bureaucratic. Zen, like Sufism after the thirteenth century, became so institutionalized that the path could be followed only in an order and under a "certified" teacher. Transmitted knowledge and mechanical observances took the place of personal experience. Its "Ho!" strike to bring enlightenment was picked up by the Japanese in the thirteenth century. This sado-masochistic buffeting reminds me of the corporal punishment meted out in British public schools, though the target there was different. Along with the cold baths, flogging was supposed to add character to the culprit. The Zen blow is motivated similarly: the sluggard is slow at satori so he is struck alongside the head.

Physicality of this ilk came to these shores with the Puritans. At the turn of the century it was going great guns in Germany. I remember reading of a Swabian slob of a schoolmaster named Hauberle and his adventures with corporal punishment. I looked up records he kept to prove that "severe constraint gives poise, self-control, and will." In 50 years this guy dished it out as follows: 911,527 blows with a cane; 124,010 with a rod; 40,989 with a ruler; 136,715 with the hand; 10,295 over the mouth; 7,905 boxes on the ear; 1,115,800 snaps on the head; and 22,763 *nota benes* with a Bible! Most of the punishment was dealt out for miscues on Bible verses.

The British loved caning also. An 18th century schoolmaster named Parr so loved to flog his charges that when they didn't misbehave he would ask to flog them anyway, promising that their next misdeed would be on the house!

Anyhow, as a sometime student of Zen, I don't think this kind of physical punishment can buy a genuine mystical breakthrough. Corporal punishment can be a corrective if done with love: watch a mama bear cuff a straying cub around. As for the *koan,* I think Zen's insistence on it is as dogmatic and silly as the Indians requiring a mantra before true "consciousness" breaks through. The *koans* don't make sense and aren't required to: "Question: Why is a cat when he flies? Answer: The higher, the fewer." This doesn't strike me as anything other than bureaucratic mysticism.

More to the point, does Zen improve fighting and, conversely, does fighting help Zen? Zen has traditionally been associated with the samurai for a good many years. And yes, Zen taught them to die well, if not always intelligently. But what interests me more is Gedo Zen (the "Outside Buddhist" way). Tempu Nakamura, a yoga adept, reportedly can make men move without himself moving or speaking. Then there's the Emma method by which one can walk on swords with the bare feet and paralyze sparrows so that they can't move. E.J. Harrison in his classic *The Fighting Spirit of Japan* mentions old *kiai* masters who could shout and birds would fall as though dead; shout again and the birds would fly away.

These abilities come from *joriki,* a power deriving from concentration. Hakuin Roshi, a famed Zen master-scholar, writes that the supra-normal skills of Gedo Zen require a heightened state of alertness initially and that this may cause strain at first, but later it disappears and only relaxed alertness remains. So possibly Zen can add to fighting technique. But does fighting help Zen? I think I answered that when I excoriated the hitting that goes with the institution. In my eyes this is impure and simple aggression. Fighting cannot help Zen, though Zen may aid some aspects of fighting. Buddhism was perverted by the warrior. The samurai, as Okakura pointed out in *The Japanese Spirit* (1909), renounced desire, not that he might enter Nirvana, but that he might acquire the contempt of life which would make him a perfect warrior.

I once was driving with an experimenter in these occult arts and he confided that by giving up sex he was able to generate heat from his hand. With that, he held his right hand up two feet from me. I immediately felt a surge of heat. But if he expected me to congratulate him for this, he was a porno star at a tantric retreat. I merely turned the car heater on full blast and asked him: "What did you say you gave up for this superfluous skill?"

## Aggression and the Martial Arts

I am often asked whether the martial arts increase or lower our aggressive tendencies? Does fighting, through its disciplines, make us more humble and pacific or does it simply strip our aggressiveness? Ideally, of course, these arts should teach self-control and moderation, but in real life they don't always do that. After all, fighting and competition are their very rationale, and this can be a fatal legacy.

Still, the martial arts are founded upon an ethic of self-defense, not aggression. We must study them in that ultimate light. Tests show that watching football increases hostility, but watching gymnastics does not. The mainland Chinese teach *wu shu* as gymnastics. Maybe we could learn from them. It bothered me to see the Chicago police in 1968 use correct Asian stick techniques on kids protesting for peace. Ironically, I was one of those teaching such techniques during that period. And I have read that Marine guards at the Great Lakes brig in July 1975 were accused of using "heart checks" on prisoners: pumping the heel of the palm against the heart. Reportedly, such acts caused at least one suicide. It's downright dispiriting. Violence and aggression have killed our national character and pushed style out of our lives. Take tennis. Have you watched the idiotic antics of Connors and McEnroe? The epitome of bad taste. You didn't see that kind of thing during tennis' palmy period of the thirties. Don Budge said of his opponent from Germany back then, Baron von Cramm, that he was the greatest gentleman (in an era of gentlemen) he'd ever seen. Not only would von Cramm not harass another player, he would never think of embarrassing an official by questioning a call.

## A Note on Judo

Jigoro Kano created judo to refine the violence of jujutsu into sportive wrestling. Although blessed with thousands of *judoka* of Japanese extraction, America has done poorly in judo. The players are outnumbered by the officials and the scene is a bureaucratic mess. The top officials usually were mediocre players who remember themselves as champions. They now maintain their positions of power at the expense of real champions. And this bureaucracy impedes real judo. America finished 26th in a recent world championship. A palpable pity.

Judo as conceived by Kano was an exquisite expression. But it has not travelled well. Now it is practiced strictly as jacketed wrestling. But it is a legitimate form of wrestling. I'd like to see it continue, embodying Kano's ideas of active gentleness, yielding, mutual help, and efficient living. Some will deny judo had these qualities even in Japan. At least in Japan the philosophical and theoretical work had been done and the practice was evolving when *shiai*—the overstress on competition—undermined it and left it as simply another wrestling form without Kano's ethic. Nor am I speaking of aesthetics—the *kata* (form display) of putting the artistic over the competitive. I'm not talking about ornament and shadow; I'm speaking of essence. The *kata* are okay to see; better to do. They should not supplement competition but complement it. I'd keep them not so much for how they look but for how they feel and what they mean. I'm speaking mainly of a judo that will have something for all age groups. It should have competition, recreation, and self-defense—all these elements. Not so competitive that it cripples those over 40; not so recreational that it frustrates youngsters wanting a real tussle; and not so self-defensive that it becomes boxing rather than wrestling. It should have a cooperative spirit; it should *reduce* ego. I remember the late great champion, Richard Fukuwa, saying once that real judo is in the bowing (courtesy) and the falling (yielding).

## Challenges

Challenges were a traditional part of the Asian martial arts. Through challenges you tested yourself and others. But that was a long time ago in a far away place. And though we're talking of Asia, challenges were not restricted to that continent. We had our own fast gun challenges. And a European code sired our own Western frontier antics. Sir William Petty (1623-87) was once challenged by a knight. Extremely short-sighted, and being the challengee, Petty had the right to name place and weapon. He nominated for the place, a dark cellar; the weapon, a great carpenter's axe. This turned the knight's challenge to ridicule, and nothing came of it.

Struthers Burt, the poet, in *My Student Days in Germany* wrote that German students were keen on the schlager and the saber, but had a horror of fists, which they considered ungentlemanly.

If you wanted to join a duelling group, you first had to fight three duels. These sabre addicts sported their facial scars as a badge of honor much as Japanese collegiate judo players flaunt their cauliflower ears derived from groundwork. In both cases it is possible to do the thing and not be disfigured, but the badge is so sought after that nearly everyone has it. In fact, there are methods to get it easily and with little or no pain. Pretty silly. Anyhow, many Germans in the period just before World War II went around provoking incidents with foreigners which would end by their challenging the other party to a duel. Most foreigners could not compete. Once, a visiting young American baseball pitcher was gulled into such a situation in a beer hall. The youngster, challenged, had the presence of mind to know that he had the choice of weapons, and promptly specified baseballs at 15 feet!

The general lunacy abroad in this land encourages the poor neurotic or psychopath to go about challenging. You encounter all kinds of weirdos in this business. Many are seeking a beating. They go about manifesting Freud's intuition of a death wish. And you don't spend your life, or shouldn't, pleasuring every aberration you meet. The onus is on you. That bird may want a beating because he's a dilly, but if you supply him the thumping you join his club.

It is passing strange but Western boxing doesn't have challenges. Here is a sport where there is unmitigated contact, but no challenges; yet in the essentially no-contact Asian regimes you have people going around challenging. This may be because the real contact in training would quickly delete these weirdos. Pain is unique: it can't be imaged. If vicarious warriors ever felt it, they might give up boxing and masochism.

I used to get challenged, but not anymore. Why? Because now I say a uniform no to all such challenges, whereas I used to be selective. I never wanted to hurt anyone, but I did want to test myself. So there was war between those two intentions. Even in the old days, however, there weren't too many challenges. People always talk as though there are many more than there are. But if the guy was psycho, I'd puff him up about what a gorgeous broth of a man he was and send him off gloriously happy. If he were fairly rational but lacking in skill, it was tougher to deter him.

A good samurai would not accept a challenge from an unskilled pip-squeak even if it meant that the guy afterward would swagger around accusing the samurai of cowardice. I played it this way. Your own ego is a worse danger than most challengers. So I'd beg off and the guy would strut with some barbecue only to be turned every way but loose the following week by some bird I had done in left-handed previously.

Now I refuse all challenges. I know when to stop. Accepting a worth-while challenge years ago was one thing; now is another. I've matured—my critics would call it aged—enough now to see the disutility in such fighting. Say the guy is good and I want to learn from him, so I agree to his challenge. I thwack him from hither to yon, remembering my old mistakes as he makes them. He slinks off. The next week sure as shooting, there'll be another one there with better credentials and we'll do another little jig. Say I beat him too; the line will only get longer and if, to save time, I take them all on at once, then the next guy up will have a knife, a gun, or a hand grenade. That's why, from a practical standpoint, I say no like good girls should.

That's *practical.* The better reason is moral. The longer I fight, the sillier it seems. Tohei, the aikido master, refuses all challenges. He regards the challenge as a game and, he says, a fight is no game. But if the miscreant were ever to visit a crime on Tohei, then the concept of self-defense—on which all these ethical forms of combat are built—would come to the fore and the attacker would lose his butt. A few years ago a couple of friends of mine, aiki students of Tohei, visited him at his *dojo* in Tokyo. The same night they were there a judo 4-*dan* sauntered in. Hostile from the beginning, he insisted on trying to bend Tohei's "unbendable arm." He tried and, mid-way through, seeing it was no-go, he arced the arm downward toward the floor. Tohei went with it and ended up in an undignified position, his body bent over, his head near the mat. The ineffable one held the posture a moment, then released it. Tohei stood up, smiled, and told the *judoka* how good he was and congratu-lated him on his technique. (Never mind that the guy had not played by the rules or that he hadn't locked or thrown Tohei). The man looked at my friends with a triumphant look and swashbuckled out of the *dojo,* the winner. But he was wrong. Tohei won going away. He could have swallowed this fish whole. But didn't. He could have dismembered this ape. But didn't. With his talons, torn this eagle from the sky. But didn't. Tohei could have put on a show for his troops and the visiting Americans, but didn't. Instead, he let himself be bent over to ridicule, possibly losing face among some of his students, rather than hurting this chap.

Some will argue that if you let it be known you don't accept challenges, this will increase the frequency of them. If you refuse a challenge, won't the maniacs then line up to make them, safe in the knowledge you'll say no? Perhaps, but you can also leave it ambiguous. Hold your head like Chanticleer and steel your eyes as you say no—as if you don't really mean it. Sort of like the girl in Pantagruel who was being swept away and who shouted no—but not too loudly.

## Tough 'Uns

Fats Waller once demurred at playing in Art Tatum's presence, saying "God is in the house tonight." Yet Tatum later said that Fats "is where I come from." Which only goes to show that there is often more than one giant around. I've met my share. Now these were all mortals. They had weaknesses. None could compete with Charles XII of Sweden who Voltaire said was the only man without any weakness. Charles wouldn't sleep in a bed and enjoyed rigor like it was luxury. He and 3,000 men beat 50,000 Russians. My boys can't compete with that but in their own ways they were pretty good. They trained hard to increase their natural endowments. They didn't have talismans or gimmicks.

I would nominate as one tough hombre, Dick Hanaka, a chap I knew in Hawaii before World War II. Since he was 15 he had been immersed up to his cauliflowered ears in the fighting trade. He started by sitting at Okazaki's knee. In a few years he excelled in that brand of ju-jutsu and could more than hold his own with the island champions who espoused the orthodox *Kodokan* style of judo. He also was responsible for the rerouting of some Japanese freighters. Japanese 4-*dans* and 3-*dans* off their ships delighted in making mincemeat of the locals—until Dick got his full growth. After he had taken down the entire team three ships running, the story goes that Japanese freighters thereafter until World War II were diverted to another, more distant, island port.

Dick didn't feel that was exceptional. The old man (Okazaki) found an oak of a guy once who was a sugar warehouseman. Biff, we called him, of course. He was 6'6" going both ways. For eight hours a day he would load 100-pound sacks of sugar using only the thumb and index finger of each hand. Because he often worked in his best suit—the girls were waiting every night—he would lift the sacks at nearly full arm extension so as not to dirty his clothes. Well, the old man had a special *gi*—more a tent—made for him, and primed him for the next load of Japanese sailors. The time came. He was first man out on our line. He grabbed the *gi* of his opponent and straightway took him up and held him over his head. Full point. Ditto to the next four men. Biff never learned a throw, didn't need to: if he got hold of you, he got you. Unfortunately, that was his first and last match. Because most of us had day jobs, we could contest only at night. For Biff this was decisive. He had to choose between judo and the girls and he felt committed to the latter. "It's not for me: it's for them," Biff would say. He was committed and he believed in good conscience he couldn't let them down.

During this period Dick often hustled for Okazaki. The master and he would visit an unsuspecting *dojo* and, while the old man over wine spoke with the manager, Dick would be taking folks from all and sundry. After an hour or so, the old man would suggest to the *sensei* a friendly bet on the respective merits of their fighters. Once the bet was agreed to, Dick would feign difficulty in tossing one of the lowliest black belts. As the bets increased, Dick's technique—*hanegoshi* (spring hip) was his best—got better. But he made sure he never won handily. By the time he got to the champion and the big bet was on, Dick was tired, as much from his fakery as from his exertions, and would take hold, immediately *ki-ai,* up the guy would go, and the host *sensei* once again would take out his nearly depleted wallet.

With all his prowess, Dick was never a bully and never mean. Once in a bar he was with a dove of a girl, fascinating enough to make him pace himself, and a rhubarb developed. Behind them four fellows began throwing fists. After a while this began to cut in on Dick's conversation so he finally asked the bartender/owner to stop the fracas. That one demurred (what can I do?) and seemed to be enjoying it, so Dick finally reached over and lifted him clear of the floor with one hand, took another swig of his beer, and reiterated the request. When the now big-eyed owner was released, he brought a 10-inch blackjack down on the bar, shouted, "That's all, boys," and the fight stopped instanter.

Leonard Gmirkin, a fry cook in Vienna, studied for years under a master of the internal in Tibet whose name he will not reveal. Gurdjieff observed once that the person who can serve tea properly can do anything. Gmirkin's experience proves the weight of those words. He believed it unnecessary to practice, getting all of it he needed at the grill. Every time he turned an egg he had circularly evaded and struck symbolically. Every time he pressed a hamburger down, some phantom's innards suffered.

I also knew a superb warrior in the wrongly named "soft art" of t'ai-chi.

Some deride this form as mere scuffling. Obviously they have never toed the scratch with a master. I was in Singapore in 1965 trying on the locals for size. Since most of them were harder than a New York landlord I was breezing through them making like a very "parfait knight." My last night they greeted me with the news that Lu Te-an, a veritable artist at pushing hands, had come out from Wuhan on the mainland to visit his parents and would drop by. I waited and around 9 o'clock he sauntered in, small and skinny, but walking firm on two good legs and lightly swinging one good arm—the other was missing! I didn't have time to wonder: the boys immediately pushed me in with him. Well, I'm used to operating against two arms and was at a loss how to proceed. Lu, smiling, proceeded for me. He touched me lightly and I richocheted off the wall. It was obvious he was trying to get my attention. He had it. I bounded back in, felt him, and unleased that good old steel straight-arrow energy. I had him all the way—except towards the last. The bang fizzled out in that last fraction of a second, I felt an expanse of air, then his hand, and off I went into the old wall. I then got nefarious and tried some aiki techniques but he neutralized these even more easily. Every plot I hatched ended on that blasted wall. I've often wondered since what Lu could have been with both arms.

America doesn't have many master fighters—I group John Wayne with Truman Capote—but there are a few. It is not widely known that I have granted a certificate of Master Fighter to some worthies. There is but one grade, pegged at the 9-*dan* level of *Kodokan* judo. So far I have certified only seven persons.

Predictably, my requirements are stiff. I select; no one applies. No money changes hands. I spend years evaluating a person; he or she must be a synthesis of skill, not a one-shot, one-act performer. Besides his own achievements, I end by levying an examination which to date has flunked 90% of the eligibles. The tests are secret but to let you sample their rigor, I cite a few.

Because there are so many strutting gamecocks at martial arts contests, I put it down early that to enter my coterie an expert had to be able to fall properly from a most undignified position. Dig this: I stack three light card-tables atop each other, place a wood stool on a chair and the chair on the top table. I seat the eligible, blindfolded, his hands tied behind him, on the stool. Then to the snappy rhythm of Fats Waller's "Up Jumped You With Love" I sweep a leg of the bottom table, bringing the eligible down in a profound fall. The combinations and permutations of falling from such a perch are infinite and few of the fish manage it adequately, much less well.

After selecting a suitably redneck town (the midwest has some good ones, the south more), I pick out its roughest bar. To qualify, the bar must have been closed down at least once for disturbing civil order in the 30 days preceding the test. I put the eligible in this bar on a Saturday night and instruct him to insult in escalating increments: (1) the bartender; (2) the region—this works wonders in the south; and (3) the U.S. military, (4) the President; and (5) professional football. If the locals are still pacific—and this seldom happens—I am there dressed and voiced as one of them and I work them up against the stranger. When they froth at the mouths, I open their cages. Here, the test starts. But it's not what you would expect. Many fighters can physical their way out of belligerent taverns, but how many can talk their way out? For that is what the test is: the eligible must walk out without touching his antagonists. Easy? You try it.

# IV

# THE CAPOEIRA CHAMPION

*"We are all going to die in a couple of hours."*
—St. Teresa of Avila

One of the most fascinating self-defense arts in the world is Brazil's *capoeiragem* (pronounced kap-oo-ay-ra-gem). I can vouch for its effectiveness. First, though, let me give some of its background.*

*Capoeira,* as it is generally called, was originated by Bantu negroes in Angola, Africa, as a religious dance. In the 16th century the slave trade brought many adepts in *capoeira* to Bahia, Recife, and Rio de Janeiro, the main centers of slave import in Brazil. The slaves practiced the movements in leisure periods. The dance induced a trance which served to allay some of the hardships they had to endure. Life for them was unmitigated torture. The colonist wanted their bodies; the Jesuits, their souls.

From this dance these poor transplanted blacks coming from parched and barbarous Angola, where natural selection was effected through an intensive exercise of force and ferocity, got release from daily toil and they got something else.

They were at the mercy of plantation overseers, often as not criminals hired out of jails, men who would abuse them and, if the whim touched them, rape their wives. And these men were armed. *Capoeira* thus evolved so that the slave got relaxation but, quite as important, he derived a method of self defense, frightening because nothing was barred. For him it was no sport but a matter often of life or death.

To escape bad conditions, slaves frequently would flee to the interior. Overseers, police, and soldiers would seek them out. Even when subdued by

---

*My main sources are Gilberto Freyre's *The Mansions and the Shanties,* 1963; Inezil Penna Marinho's *Subsidios Para a Historia da Capoeiragem no Brasil,* 1956; L. P. DaCosta's *Capoeiragem,* no date; *Capoeira* (photos by Marcel Boutherot), 1963; and *O Jugo da Capoeira,* 1955.

superior force, however, the *capoerista* was not out of it. Shackled, he often was able to escape again by using his legs and head.

After the quashing of the republic, *capoeira* developed into a form of self-defense on farms and in towns. It was assimilated by mulattos, who as mixtures (according to Marinho) had more agility than the whites.

Freyre writes of the urbanized *capoeirista*:

> ". . . his specialty was his razor or knife; his trademark, the kinky hair combed in the shape of a turban, the light sandals on his feet, which were almost those of a dancer, and his loose-jointed gait. His art included, in addition to all of this, a variety of difficult steps and movements of incredible agility, in which the street vagabonds were initiated almost as in a Masonic rite . . . experts in the use of daggers and knives but, above all, in head-butting, tripping, and kicking the feet out from under an adversary."

Besides this, they used witchcraft and poisons against their enemies.

*Capoeira* reached its apex in the nineteenth century; the transmigration of the Portuguese court was one of its most hectic periods. More than 15,000 invaded Rio, plundering. They robbed even the Chief of Police who was beaten when he made the mistake of not carrying enough money on him.

The civil police constabulary created in 1808 failed to cope with the *capoeirista*, necessitating establishment of the military police under Major M. N. Vidigal. This force, however, failed to stop the fighters and even allied with them later to put down German and Irish mercenaries who were sacking the city. In 1821 fines were levied against the practice of *capoeira* but in 1831 it came to the fore again and contributed to the ouster of Don Pedro I.

Later, during the long reign of Don Pedro II, *capoeira* was freely practiced by commoners and gentry alike. In the war against Paraguay, many *capoeirista* distinguished themselves in hand-to-hand combat at the front. In the decline of the empire these men played an important role fighting on the Republican side.

Under the Republic, however, a new phase in persecution of *capoeira* began with a decree of October 11, 1890, which prescribed a prison term of 15-20 days for practicing it. By then *capoeiristas* were a real power in society and the cause of much bloodshed. They formed powerful groups such as the Ganoas and the Guayamos and often fought each other. S. Ferraz, Chief of Public Security at that time, waged a concentrated campaign against them. Some *capoeiristas* were used to entrap others. If taken by surprise by others with fast reflexes, such fighters would reveal themselves by using *capoeira* and be imprisoned.

Ferraz successfully deported many fighters and drove the art out of the streets into formal parlors. One outstanding fighter, Jose Elisio dos Reis, a member of an eminent family, was deported in 1890, causing a crisis in the Brazilian cabinet.

In this century many fighters went into the army and travelled widely (even to Japan) giving exhibitions of the form. In 1907 the earliest brochure on *capoeira, O Guia do Capoeira on Ginastica Brasileira* (Guide to *Capoeira* or Brazilian Gymnastics), appeared. Later *capoeira* was systematized into a sport and in 1928 Anibal Burlamaqui published a pamphlet entitled *Ginastica Nacional (Capoeiragem) Metodizada e Regrada (National Gymnastics—Capoeira — Systematized and Amended)* which is reportedly the best book on the art.*

Today, tourists in Bahia hotels can read signs "*Capoeira* today; see porter for reservations." And when they go to the sheds where these dances are given, they will hear music from the *berimbau*, a bow-shaped instrument hit by a small stick and plucked with a coin; the *caxixi*, a bamboo and wicker rattle also held by the *berimbau* player; and by tambourines. The dance features alternate attacking and defending. And some of it is done very slowly. The classical Angolan method features movements done, à la t'ai-chi, in slow motion to emphasize the grace that comes from years of study and practice.

Lest it become simply a thing of modern dance, *capoeiristas* maintain a few of the old combative schools and, inevitably, many frauds cashing in on the world karate craze. One of the best teachers is M. Machado (popularly known as Master Bimba), a black battler now in his seventies who has a school in Bahia (Brazilians say Christ was born in Bahia). Legendary in Bahia, Machado once defeated three rivals in an afternoon and his school has flourished since the mid-30's.

Bahia now has 36 *capoeira* gyms, Rio and Sao Paulo, 30 each, and there are several in state capitals like Recife and Belo Horizante. Some term *capoeira* a national sport.

But if it is, what is it? Machado incorporated judo and other arts into his method. Some old-timers don't like this. Another kind of dance purist decries contact in favor of folklore and dance. In 1973 I went down there to see for

---

*Reading this chapter made my own publisher aware of *capoeira*, and he found one of the senior disciples of Mestre Bimba living and teaching in San Francisco. The result: an inspired manuscript by a living *capoeirista*! It is now available from North Atlantic Books as: *Capoeira: A Native Brazilian Art Form* by Bira Almeida.

myself the genuine *capoeira*.

I had seen it in the 1940's and 1950's but this time I had a good contact, a professor who owed me a big courtesy, and he put me on to one of the last real *capoeiristas*, Guy Ruiz. Arriving in Bahia in what must have been the hottest weather ever endured by man, I set about seeing him.

Even with an introduction it wasn't easy to find Ruiz. But when I finally ran him down, I found a pleasant, smiling, thoroughly ugly man in his 50's. His house was simple. He lived alone, his wife having died some years before.

He knew of my mission and agreed to tell me anything I wanted to know, but joked: "There's a lot of *capoeira* around for you to see. Why do you come to me?"

I told him politely that I had seen tourist *capoeira*. It didn't impress me. I wasn't a tourist, a folklorist, or a modern dancer. I was interested in the evolution of distinct fighting systems and *capoeira* was one of the most unique. He had the reputation, I said, of being possibly the greatest exponent of the art in the world.

He modestly threw up his hands. "No, no, let us say I continue to practice what I learned from infancy."

On that we had some excellent wine, then went out in back to look at his orchids which he tended like a mother hen.

And then he started delineating *capoeira*. His English was better than my Portuguese, so we communicated in it.

"The tourist," he began, "sees dancers who spend most of their time on their hands rather than their feet."

At this he dived into the air and came down into a perfect handstand, his body supported perfectly by his arms with not a tremor in the muscle.

"That is the influence of the dance. And it's not bad or non-functional."

He stood up by flipping up and back, landing gracefully on his feet.

"*Capoeira* has cartwheels, somersaults, and all sorts of what one would call extreme body movements. Please remember that, though some may appear too fancy for use, many are useful and all of them enhance one's mobility."

He dived then on to one arm, held it as before and snapped up out of it.

"For mobility is all-important," he said. "Our oppressors were usually bigger, much bigger, and if we were in any way static we would have been crushed by their superior strength.

"In fact, in the old days we used a trick so as to avoid detection when the police were looking for us. We'd sidle up to our quarry and pull his hat down over his eyes before attacking him (similar to the *metsubishi*, or 'blinder', taught in Japanese combatives, in which you slap the opponent before using your main technique). This was pretty good but had one defect—you had to be close to the man to pull it off. That's why only the most skilled of us ever used it. If it misfired, the fellow would have you in his big arms.

"Thus our stuff is generally not of the close variety but dynamically long range. Because it is spectacular some may call it reckless. It isn't. We have an old *golpe* (strike) which we call *solta*: you butt your antagonist in the belly with your head. Many think it is our prime technique. In truth, it was used mainly in slave times; it was an accepted technique when your hands were tied or your fingers broken. The art hadn't been refined then. The technique naturally developed because slaves had strong neck muscles from carrying great bundles of *mate*, bundles often weighing more than 300 pounds, slung over one's back and supported by a band around the forehead. But, if the *solta* misses, it robs you of a covering defense. For this reason we seldom use it." *

I pointed out to him that even if well-targeted the *solta* would be a hazardous undertaking against a western boxer with a good uppercut.

"Quite," he said. "And even though we don't train with that kind of competition in mind, we try to make the art as perfect as we can. It has to be. For in Brazil a gun or a knife was once considered a fair weapon and there was no shame if you were wounded or killed. But to hit a man with your fists or feet, as we do, was a supreme insult and he would use any means to avenge it.

"We have about everything you need for complete self-defense. Grappling, no — for the reasons I gave earlier. We could not compete with our bigger antagonists on this score."

Guy then went through his repertoire. On the *pantana* he adroitly kicked me under the chin, going up on his toes like a football punter, but reserving his power.

"Now, you may say that the *pantana* is too high and too risky, but notice how quickly I do it, which precludes your grabbing my leg, and notice, too, that I am still frontal to you and my eyes never leave you.

"Forget the *solta* and the *pe de fogo*."

I interrupted to ask what the latter meant.

---

*Football players in the U.S. use a technique of "hitting them in the numbers" by spearing with the hard plastic helmet. It is the chief cause of football injuries and, ironically, injures those using it (the neck and spine especially) more than it does the intended victims. Perhaps they could stand some proper *solta* practice or work carrying bundles of *mate*. Weird — the projectile is damaged more than the target. But there are many weird things about this business miscalled a sport or game; happily, the subject is outside our province.

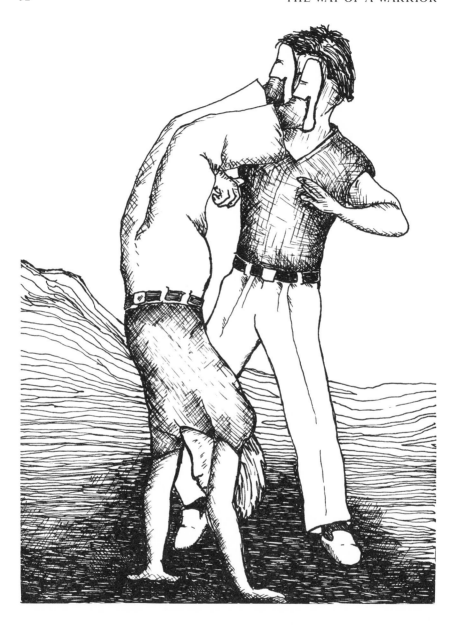

*Capoeira's Back High Kick*

"It translates as 'flaming foot'", he said, "and perhaps was actually used in olden times. If so, the attrition rate must have been high. The *capoeirista* timed it so that he would kick the overseer's gun from his hand just as it discharged. Thus the name."

"During its heyday, the art was a complete science. We used feints such as *lamparina* (face slap), *cocara* (cheek scratch), and *cusparada* (spit-in-the-eye) to turn a man into our kicks.

"If struck on the ground we would use a *tesoura,* a knee-ankle scissors and would often fake a fall to get an opponent with this trick. It usually worked.

"Sure, we took risks with such a wide variety of techniques, we always had a chance. I have said we avoid closing with an opponent. But this doesn't mean we are afraid to go in. Here, stand there a moment."

I stood. He feinted a right foot, then the left hand, and then almost faster than the eye could follow he dived between my legs, landing in a crouch. Before I could move away he arose, spilling me onto the ground.

"That," he said, briskly, "we call the *corta-capim.* But our most spectacular is the *rabo-de-arraia* named after the thorny-spined sting-ray fish."

Here Guy sprang upside down on his hands and in the same movement thrust both of his heels at my jaw, stopping, luckily for me, an inch short of the target.

"This trick," he said, "we used sparingly, but it was so effective that we never had to hold razor blades between our toes as some people have reported."

Guy's movements were beautifully fluid. He was the prettiest ugly man I ever saw. He circled smoothly into roundhouse kicks *(pontapes)*, snapped into flying dropkicks *(voo de morsego)*, and slithered hither and yon with straight jabs *(pisadas)* using me as the target. Those incomparable feet missed me, often by just an intentional hair's-breadth.

"Now, you may say that this is all very virile, graceful, and even functional. But without contact for me it is meaningless."

He paused and, despite the skill he had shown, I was half happy, thinking it was an invitation to the dance. But no.

He said, "There are some masters now in Brazil who feel a lack in the old *capoeira*. So they bring judo, karate, and tactics from other methods into the old *capoeira*. But to me it has always been a complete art: what it lacked it didn't need. Synthesis is too often merely a dilution. So what I wish to do is to take the old *solta*, the head-butt of my ancestors, also called the *cabecada* and *cabeza*, teach it to you, and then let you use it full-force on my belly."

"Why should you do that?" I asked. I was worried about injuring him (after all, such a blow, unopposed, can be mortal) but I didn't want to betray my worry.

But he saw it and he laughed. "I don't want to give away the plot," he said, "so I will only tell you that you need not worry for me. Why do I do it? Because it is a tradition with me to take anything I give out. Too many *capoeirista* can dish it out but they capsize the first time they are hit. If one is able to absorb another's strikes without fear of injury then he can put proportionally more effort into attack and less into defense. So that is why I let you do this."

With that, sweat oozing from the pair of us, he gave me a half-hour drill on the nicety—and variety—of the *solta*.

Apparently I was a good student.

"For a combative man," he mused aloud during one pause, "you are extremely open to learning something new: and for a big man you are quite agile at it."

I was so taken with this praise that I thought he might wish to back away from his offer, and politely told him that it was enough for me to learn the *solta*. Graciously I let him know that there was no need for him to be struck by it. After all, I couldn't return the hospitality — I sure as hell wasn't going to let him have a clean shot at me with it.

He laughed at this. "Mr. Gilbey, you must not continue worrying on my account. It makes you seem a fussbudget."

*That* silenced me and we went back to practice. And, in jig time, I had it down brown and he put his small frame (5′3″, 130 pounds) out in front of me where I could get at it and told me to heave ho.

I remember well the tableau: sweat glistened on him and ran in rivulets down me.

"Do as you wish with what you have learned of the *solta*," he said, "and don't be concerned with counters. I won't use any. I merely want to show you that it is possible for a well-trained man to take this. Don't think me immodest, but no one else in Brazil can do this."

This was enough for me. So John F. Gilbey, student of the manic tendency in humans called fighting, scholar of the human body and its efficient functioning, veteran of as many street fights as there are streets in a small city, took off toward the waiting figure. I took two giant steps, lowered the 20 percent of me called my head. As my left foot touched ground, it acted as a catapult, shooting my body like a projectile into his hospitable gut.

Even if he could have absorbed the shock of it, the force alone should have knocked him back. It didn't. I hit him and ricocheted off like water off a duck's back. I lay half-stunned. After all, I had given it my all and it hurt. My neck felt like it was broken and, at the opposite pole, strangely, both my ankles were twinging with excruciating pain.

But Ruiz stood there undisturbed. Smiling, saying nothing. He waited for me to get up.

I did, but not without some creaking. "That," I said, once vertical, "was a helluva demonstration. I think I'm hurt worse than you."

Immediately he was all compassion, but I shrugged my pains off as transient and of no cause for concern. I was still feeling them a month later.

We had dinner then, a spicy repast prepared by a little brown man who had arrived unnoticed by me and whose only visible sign until he brought in his culinary delights smacking of pre-World War II Hunan and Szechuan was a battered old cardboard suitcase parked at the edge of the house.

"My friend," Ruiz said as the man spread the dishes, "comes in once a year or so to cook for me. He is a real master of it." The old gent beamed at this and scurried out.

"But," Ruiz went on, "he lives in Mexico and doesn't make the trip for that purpose alone. He only pretends to. I believe he comes to look at my art. And perhaps learn enough of it to oralize it. For I'm told that he is something of a charlatan and has fooled American anthropologists into believing he is a warrior sage. In reality he is nothing but a cook."

"But," I put in, chewing on some residue of Vesuvius, "a darned good one."

I told him of the chow-mein cooks now teaching kung-fu and the young and old Indians posing as gurus abroad in America.

"That is always the way," he mused sadly, "those who know not, teach, and those who know are unknown."

We continued talking as we stoked up. He told me that he had beaten nine state *capoeira* champions in one day. How many at one time? Here he said that there were seven or so troublemakers who had insulted his wife in a tearoom once and he had physically cleared the room in a minute and a half.

"But," he drawled, "I don't like to fight. I only like to exercise my art. Particularly for someone like you who can really appreciate it."

At this he abruptly pushed the table a few inches forward loving the way—I could see it in his eyes—I neutralized it, rose, and said, "Shall we have a go?"

Put me down as a coward (but don't let me hear it), as a cringing mass of flesh, as too much of a cognitive, thinking reed, but I must confess I turned down the offer — well, okay — challenge.

I was well-fed, well-muscled, and well-trained in a hundred unscrupulous methods of flushing men down physical drains but I still said "No Thanks". I knew what *capoeira* comprised and it didn't frighten me. But thinking of Guy

Ruiz's mastery of the movements of this superb art and of his body's ability to take any kind of strike, I quickly decided "what the hell."

Or maybe it's just that I'm getting older (and smarter) or maybe I really was afflicted with the quick dose of what we used to call "Delhi Belly" (diarrhea). I dunno. But anyhow I used the latter excuse and Ruiz seemed regretful but assured me he understood.

And that is how I came to crawl away from the champion *capoeirista* of this century.

# V

# THE WOMAN WHO COULDN'T BE RAPED

*"Men wear out, but a woman is a woman as long as she lives."*

—Moms Mabley

Man is physically inferior to most animals. George Shaller once counted 155 copulations by a male gorilla in 55 hours. Casanova, Don Juan, and Jack Johnson (his recipe for staying in there was "Fried eels and distant thoughts") couldn't begin to compete with this. Stronger even than the male gorilla is the female who in that same period serviced several other males besides our friend. So there's something to be said for the female homo sapiens being stronger than the male. In some ways, only. The female simply can't compete with the male in tests of raw strength. Moreover, because of her anatomy, she should not box western style. I hear that recently they've started girl boxing in ever-backward Texas. And the trend is spreading.

To put it plain: women can't fight. And shouldn't. A woman trained properly can function well in self-defense. However, the bilge in the Sunday supplements on milady knocking the 250-pound thug down is silly. Even with the quality of mugging down 300 percent since the thirties, few women should try to confront a male antagonist. If he wants your purse, give it to him, etc. etc. What "etc." may not cover is rape.

The one constant that researchers have found in rapists is that they are excessively violent. This being so, if a woman can psychologically handle it, she might be better served submitting or pretending to faint. If she resists by trying her lady karate, it might anger him and push his psychotic violence too far. For there is none quite so erratically savage as a rapist. Years ago a friend on the Chicago detective force told me that their operating procedure on coming upon a rape in an alley was to throw rocks at the rapist to get him clear of his victim and then take him. If challenged while doing his thing he was apt to kill the victim.

I know these words will enrage feminists who view rape as a political as well as a physical crime. I grant the ladies that all too often the rape victim in America is treated worse than the rapist, but granting that doesn't change my view of how dangerous the rape situation is for a female. I met a kung fu lass once who was bra-less (which was nice) and mindless (which wasn't). I put the question to her: she (all of 110 pounds) is on Main Street at high noon and accosted by a 300-pound monster who announces he is going to rape her there and then. The behemoth has a wooden leg which prevents him pursuing a tortoise. What would she do?

Eyes flashing, she doubled her pink fists which any worthwhile mugger would gobble at a gulp and said: "I'd let him come in and hit him twice and kick him once."

Why not run? I suggested.

"Because," she said, "I wouldn't want to give a man the satisfaction of making me run!" There you are, a woman who'd literally die for a political idea. It is ironic that many of the militant women in the martial arts tend to adopt the same machismo they justly despise in men. They should realize that swaggering hypermasculinity is a form of theatrical parody rather than evidence of real toughness. *Yin* and *yang* are a continuum running through both sexes and just as there are true men who are graceful, sensitive, and gentle, there are real women who are tough in the truest sense of the word. Many live in rugged country like Idaho and Alaska and can shoot straight, butcher hogs, and ride like bandits. These have no need to mimic men. And, as you know, the most womanly woman, if her child is threatened, will respond like a wolverine.

You can see the worst aspect of women in the martial arts in the horrid books some of them write. This is from one on female self-defense: "A quick jab from a petite female can cause more damage than a blow from a fist-swinging male. This is because your power is not derived from brute strength but from the velocity of the blow. To be powerful you must reject the old myths about female frailty and passivity and act with vigor." Forgive me ladies, but this is bilge. I suggest that a woman using kung fu/karate half-correctly against an intent rapist is in far greater danger than one who knows no self-defense.

In summary, let me revert to Chinese cosmology. There is a *yang* and — thank God! — there is a *yin.* This is, it seems to me, an ideal arrangement. The sex act itself is a crucial and lovely part of this arrangement. And however much some men — the *Playboy* types — and some women may try to distort and pervert it, nature will protect it. If women want to learn self-defense, more power to them, as long as they respect their natures and recognize their limitations.

Her name is Muffin Baxter and she lived in Galveston and studied judo for ten years with Tim Baxter before she married the lucky lug. Tim, a fourth degree black belt, went beyond sport judo and added the *atemi* (vital points) attacks and prohibited holds of jujutsu to make a well-rounded street method. Muffin learned all of this. And, by virtue of their marital relationship, she was able to learn additional tricks too intimate for Tim to divulge to other women students. This, as we shall see, was to stand her in good stead.

Muffin was a good looking gal, but sensible. She didn't flirt any more than most happily married women do. And she didn't wear high-heels or other silly garb in the street. Nonetheless, three rape attempts were made on her. Tim told me the stories, embellishing nothing—Muffin was at his elbow—not too many years ago.

The first time occurred following a party Muffin attended with a girl friend, Ann, and Ann's fiance (this was before Muffin's marriage). Some hours after dropping her, Ann's fiancee knocked on Muffin's door. He innocently wanted to discuss Ann and his relationship. Muffin let him in, prepared to do the Ann Landers bit. But this Lothario was direct and not given to small talk. He barged in, got Muffin wedged against a wall, and told her what he intended to do. She tried to dissuade him but a rollicking right hand slap to her face let her know that talking wasn't going to do it. The slap caught her in mid-sentence and really shocked her, what with 200 pounds behind it. The boy was intent and intense. Tasting blood, after a moment when the room had stopped spinning, Muffin went into a routine she had vicariously practiced many times. And it was not a *kiai* and a hack with a slender hand.

"Why fight it?" Muffin said instead and put up her arms for the embrace. But she was better than that. She added: "Come and get it, bozo." And bozo did. Nearly swooning with anticipation he trotted on into the circle of her arms. But it was her circle and she did things within and with it. She raised her left foot and put it down toed-out and with the momentum generated swung her right knee upward into his genitalia. He gave a grunt and plopped to one knee, breaking the kneecap. After driving the knee almost vertically—the closer he is, the better this technique works—into him she swung it behind his right leg and, lunging forward, attempted *osoto* (a rearward reap against his right leg). But this didn't work because his body had slumped forward so low she couldn't reap it. But it was unnecessary. She phoned the security guard downstairs at the desk and when he got there the guy still was playing "statue with genuflection" on the floor. With his busted knee, he had a bad time walking out but finally managed it, helped considerably by the none-too-delicate tugs of the burly guard. Lightning does strike twice: a year later, working overtime at her office, she was forced to use the same technique on her boss!

So much for social rape. The third defies easy categorization. Maybe you could call it judo rape. This occurred after Muffin's marriage to Tim. Well, Tim was out of town one night and Muffin taught a woman's class at the *dojo*, completing it at 9 p.m. A male nidan (second black belt), a hulk of a guy who was expected to go far in the Texas championships that year, sauntered in and watched the last half of the class. When the members left he stayed on, jawing with Muffin on judo matters. She made the mistake of inviting him to the back room for tea. Halfway through the first cup, his conversation shifted suddenly to sex and before she knew it he was advancing on her. Muffin thought quickly. A groin attack on this man was out of the question, and he would have eaten off any hand strike at the wrist. So, again, she pretended to go along. After a couple of frantic kisses, they got down to their undies. By this time he was frisky as hell but she suddenly demurred, teasingly, wondering if he could "take" her *shime* (choke).

He laughed. "Try it, be my guest," he said, putting on a judo jacket.

Muffin knelt behind him and essayed a lapel choke from the rear. He had almost no neck, his shoulders seeming to give way to his head without anything in between. But, desperate, she tried. He didn't bat an eye and merely smiled: his carotids were deep inside the hard leather of his neck. Unfeeling, he finally said: "I'm tired of this game," and began to extricate himself.

At that Muffin took her big gamble. From the kneeling posture she jumped into *dojime* (waist squeeze) throwing her legs around his middle and crossing them in front of him. Then she began to exert pressure. By this time he had almost broken the choke anyhow so she suddenly released it and grabbed his hair near his forehead with both hands and pulled back. He could have chinned in and beaten that but by then the *dojime* was affecting his innards, so he forgot the head and thrashed about trying to get free of those coiled squeezing legs.

There is a legend about an unbeatable female Chinese boxer who promised to marry any male boxer who could get her legs apart (this is a tough trick against even an untrained woman provided she isn't struck in the process). Tough as this is, the *nidan's* plight was worse: Muffin's legs were involved dynamically. He was in a vise, could not shed her and—worse—couldn't stop

*Muffin Cranks on the Waist Vise*

the pressure as it inexorably increased. She owned him.

Anyone who thinks that there is no hold a woman can sustain on a man doesn't know *dojime*. It is out of the jujutsu tradition but was so dangerous it was the only hold barred in the (almost) anything-goes matches before 1880 in Japan. Judo of course has never permitted it. It works better from the front, but Muffin would have had to contend with his arms in that position.

It didn't matter: she had him and, in excruciating pain, he knew it. He stopped thrashing momentarily and begged her to desist. But she had no option — if she had let him up he might have killed her. So she continued the pressure and shortly something went inside, bringing a scream from the man. He wilted then and was a moaning heap as Muffin dialed the police. Just then Tim walked in and she wearily put down the receiver and told him: "Honey, why don't you stay home and protect your wife like most men do?" Then laughed like hell, adding: "Now I know why they banned *dojime*."

Some time later in discussing it he told her that frontal *dojime* was more effective and she chided him: "But what would you have thought catching me in that position?" A fun-loving, disciplined pair. As I said before, I have reservations on the ability of most women to thwart rape. But where Muffin's concerned I almost sympathize with the poor rapist.

VI

# GOOD VERSUS EVIL

> *"I agree with the Bible that if you aren't
> quick, you might be dead."*
> —Red Burns

I believe that man is inherently good, but, like everyone, I see a helluva lot of evil. Camus couldn't explain the evil—so don't expect me to. It's there, that's all. Though I believe that good dominates, I have to own to the fact that I've experienced evil like you wouldn't believe. This is hardly surprising in a field that lays bare man's most aggressive tendencies. After all, to a man whose only tool is a hammer, everything tends to look like a nail.

Good is present and explained by God; Evil is present and remains unexplained. Listen.

Charlie Savage was master of the physical joke. Sometimes he was savage, but more often he was Charlie—as in "good time Charlie." Smiling most of the time, he liked physical jokes and he was also an accomplished raconteur of dirty jokes.

But this didn't make Charlie a dirty old man. He would stand behind the bar cracking dirty jokes one minute and the next protect some poor girl from being rumpled by an over-anxious longshoreman. He was married to a wisp of a gal named Edna. They were a spirited and harmonious pair but sometimes the spirit overcame the harmony and then Charlie met his match. Edna would tell him off and he'd sulk away in silence. Not to cheat, mind you, but only to try to win back what he had lost by trying to get her sympathy. It never worked.

Once in the old judo days, they'd had a rhubarb. The chill had been on a day or so when he got up on the day of the annual *shiai* (match) and ate a quiet breakfast with her. She believed, with Kin Hubbard, the Indiana humorist, that the man who has to get his breakfast downtown is apt to be late for supper. She packed his judo gear, he grabbed it and stonewalled out.

When he got down to the civic center and started to put on his *gi* (uniform), he found she'd dyed it a baby pink. Here is the mark of the man and the marriage: he split a gut laughing, put it on, and demolished his opponents, then went home where two laughing idiots fell into each other's arms. They laughed so loud and long it almost interfered with the ensuing lovemaking.

Charlie practiced judo for several years. He was big enough to be brutish, but wasn't. And too big to be fast, but was. He was never thrown and seldom beaten and would have been even better if he could have submitted to the peculiar discipline in L.A. dojos (gyms) in the mid-30's. But he was too independent, cerebral, and fun-loving to kow-tow to the *nisei* optometrists, druggists, and gardeners who lorded it over the *dojo.*

Natural power and the humor went together. In 1936 on the occasion of the visit to the U.S. by Jigoro Kano, the creator of judo, Charlie got matched up with the Japanese ace Sekine. This bird was as burly as Charlie and the day of the match all the Japanese in L.A. flooded in to see the Caucasian finally tossed. It didn't happen. They took hold and Sekine blasted in for a shoulder throw. Charlie thrust out with a hip like a wall and stopped the technique. He tapped Sekine on the shoulder and said, "A little more left hand and faster." The more Sekine attacked, the more Charlie talked and vice versa. Sekine whipped in on an *haraigoshi* (sweeping loin throw); Charlie blocked it, grabbed his leg and ran the hopping Sekine off the mat directly at the seated Kano party. Charlie held him just short of a collision and said, "How do you say 'wheelbarrow technique' in Japanese?"

Then, after they restarted in the middle, Charlie commented, "I know you don't understand my lingo but I have to tell you anyhow. You are too bulky to do *harai* with a whip. Try a more direct approach and you'll score more." And so on. Well, Charlie didn't have the skill to throw or pin Sekine and he lost the decision, but no one ever had more fun losing.

Charlie had once been a fireman on the Great Northern, B.D.—before diesels. Scooping coal had hardened him and given him the solid but fluid hip action so useful to him later.

He liked to talk about railroading.

"We've forgotten how to live. If we want to go someplace we jump on an airplane and exist. On a train you could relax and live; there was a lot of romance in it. A thrush's song in the evening, a lake lapping on stones, or coffee perking at 5 A.M. These are all great sounds. But none compare with the sound of an old steam engine's whistle at midnight. It's a pity kids can't hear it anymore.

"How'd you like firing?" I asked.

"Fine. It took a lot of muscle, but technique and headwork too. You really didn't throw that mountain of coal in off your shovel—you distributed it. You had to; if your fire was uneven the steam gauge would fall and you'd be in trouble. That was technique. Balancing inputs of water and fire took a good head but after awhile you got a feel for it. Then that became technique.

"Engineers were like the engines they drove. Flinty, picayune, testy, most of them, and then along came a sweetheart of a guy who compensated for the boors."

On the railroad or behind a bar, Charlie was a street-fighter *par excellence* and his reputation was deserved. He would fight a grizzly and give him first bite. Sure, there were a lot of stories of things that didn't happen or were inflated. There always are. But all you have to know to evaluate him is that he owned the nicest tough bar in Los Angeles. Located where the dregs of society lived, it was a place where sado-masochism, with the sado prevailing, could have taken over. But it didn't. Charlie saw to that.

His philosophy was like Dashiell Hammet's Continental Op. "Ordinarily, I am inclined to peace. The day is past when I'll fight for the fun of it, but I've been in too many rumpuses to mind them much. Usually nothing very bad happens to you, even if you lose. I wasn't going to back down just because this big stiff was meatier than I. I've always been lucky against the large sizes."

He insisted that you drink to be happy, not to fight. And then if you still wanted to bounce a couple off your neighbor, he'd shake you a bit till your eyes rolled and you laughed. The laugh might be coerced and a bit insincere at first, but soon you'd be infected by his happiness and you'd mean it.

Charlie had to be tough to stay ahead of his clientele. These roughhouse types all had tricks they wanted to try. One lumberjack would push his thumbs into your carotids (the two major arteries on the sides of the neck) to achieve paralysis. Actually this inhibition of the vagus nerve has long been used by certain stage hypnotists for quick trances. Its only drawback is that it often produces a headache in the "subject" as well. Johnnie Coulon, the old bantam champ who trained Tony Zale, used "leverage" at or near this point in his trick of withstanding the lift of any man in the audience at boxing shows in the 1930's and 1940's. Coulon claimed only one man ever lifted him off the ground and he only by sneaking up on him from the rear. He conveniently forgets the time I raised him three times in a row in Chicago in 1942 by simply hardening my neck (*I* was never choked out in judo competition), thus neutralizing Coulon's leverage.

Well, pretty much the same thing happened to the lumberjack. He advertised that he could paralyze anyone with the thumbs in the carotids.

And he got everyone—except Charlie.

Charlie's neck was rawhide over stone and the guy's thumbs just wouldn't penetrate (needless to say, readers should not experiment with pressure of any kind on the carotids!).

Charlie was also supreme at arm wrestling. Undefeated, he was so good he would let members of the Los Angeles Rams football team take on *both* his arms simultaneously and still they lost.

In later days, the karate/kung fu craze pleasured Charlie no end. He thought it was the same old violence he'd handled for years but now under a faddish label. Many times he'd had to stop erstwhile black dragons from harming each other and several times these champions tried to vent their spleen on him.

"Most of 'em can't fight," he told me, "but some think they can. As sport I guess these systems are okay, if somewhat artificial. But in a real go they encounter two things they're not trained for: pain and proximity. On pain—you can't make an omelet without breaking eggs. And you can't serve dinner without some time having lunch forced on you. You dig?"

I nodded and he continued.

"Just as bad as their inability to take pain is their inadequacy up close. And that's crucial because, as you know Johnny, that's where most brawls occur. If standing back and snapping kicks out from long distance were all of fighting, then they'd be princes. But in close quarters where they have no distance for leverage, they collapse. That's why an accomplished streetfighter can usually handle them without trouble."

I smiled and said, "Remember the Continental Op and how, when he is confronted by a big 'un wanting to try conclusions but outside where there's more space, the Op gets up, pushes his chair back with a foot and quotes Red Burns at him: 'If you're close enough, there's room enough.' "

"Right," he said. "Red Burns was a real man and a master of the close-in stuff. He was one powerful brawler and a real artist against bung starters, pool cues, and busted bottles. He gave me some sage advice once: 'Get down on the flat of your feet and punch for the belly.'"

The tough-sensitive mix he was, meant that every time Charlie had been forced into a fight—which was every time he fought—he felt guilty afterward. These agonies of remorse would really get him, so much so that after awhile he'd go to any lengths and depths to avoid fights. Sometimes he would almost run away or jokingly plead cowardice.

I remember being with him once in a tiny tavern in San Francisco. A young kung fu champ trying to win his spurs in a local tong came in looking for big guys (some of these pathetic sadists specialize in big ones). Charlie was the biggest in the place so kung-fu sat next to him at the bar and shouldered him. Charlie quickly moved to the next stool. Kung-fu slid over and shouldered him again—or tried to. But this time Charlie relaxed his shoulder and pulled it into his belt and kung-fu fell on his face. This didn't please him and he stormed up on his feet. By then three of us had hold of Charlie. But, no one thought to get the other bird and bang!, he got a right on Charlie's jaw.

Now all this time Charlie was fighting with himself. And he'd tried to yield and it hadn't worked. So, hamstrung as he was by us, he swung his massive right paw, tossing me (who had the misfortune of having hold of that arm) in the air, and decking kung-fu.

As kung-fu got up and rushed toward him, Charlie began an abject apology. "Look, I'm sorry, I didn't mean it. I'll never do it again. You're a nice guy . . ."

The shocked kung-fu stopped, incredulous, then asserted his ego by saying, "And tough."

Charlie went along. "Tough. Right, hard as nails. I'm sorry this happened. I didn't know what I was doing. You're a nice young guy, strong and in good shape. I'm old and if I fool with you I'll end up in the hospital."

As he whined his apology, the other two guys with us were so sickened by the sight and sound they were veering toward vomit. But I had seen it before and knew that everything was copacetic. Charlie's act was worthy of Barrymore. The thing now rested with kung-fu.

But he bungled it. Kung-fu got bigger as Charlie wallowed in reproach and fear. And finally said, "Okay, I'll let you off this time. But don't let it happen again. It'll teach you not to fool with a kung-fu expert."

That did it. Or rather undid it. Charlie didn't think much of kung-fu and, as he'd seen it practiced, didn't think it even deserved to be called a fighting art. (Years later when he saw some real Chinese boxing he changed his mind.)

He came out of his cringe. "Kung-fu, eh? Well that's different. Let's adjourn to the sidewalks."

The wrenching that kung-fu's mind had gone through in all this probably unsettled him, but out on the pavement he tried hard.

Charlie said again, "Kung-fu, huh? Well I'm going to use one of your own techniques on you. A style a demented Kwangsi junglelander taught me once called "The Cape Buffalo".

And in the water buffalo went. Kung-fu got a good clean shot at him as he powered in but it was like throwing a pebble at a locomotive. It sure as hell didn't deter Charlie. He didn't go into kung-fu—he went through him. The thing ended there and I spent several hours beering with Charlie talking him out of those damned recriminations.

If Charlie Savage's name did not fit him in every particular, Steve Evel's did. It is hard to get words that could describe the man. If his surname is altered a bit, say to Evil, then we have come a long way toward depicting him. Some may argue that it is cheating to take a family name and change it by a letter even to connote the abysmal badness of a man. But this man they didn't know. I did. There just is no separating a man named Evil from the worst meaning of the word "Evil": thus, I call him Evil here.

Maybe "demonic" would describe him. But Evil wasn't hyperactive—he lounged like he had invented languor. He made Robert Mitchum look like the peripatetic "Cuddles" Kissinger, he of the corrugated hair and massive ego. Drinking helped. He was a funny guy. He'd take a drink and then maybe wouldn't have another for ten minutes. He had no favorite drink, he'd drink anything—even hair tonic, so long as there was a hint of alky in it.

I never knew where Evil got the money to indulge this addiction. He had no visible means of support—no friends, male or female. It was just him and the bottle. He held the stuff well, but there was always so much of it in him that he staggered around like a canoe trying to navigate in a typhoon.

This fooled people, particularly in a new town where he wasn't known. The toughies would watch him warming a groundhog sandwich over a tarpaper fire out by a rail siding, drunk as hell. He looked eminently rollable and the boys often would try—once. But that old drunk sleeping it off under the "California blankets" (old newspapers), if kicked or even touched, was like an atomic pile going critical. More than once the police found him sodden and asleep on the yellow line of an interstate highway and more than once, they tell me, he got hit with no damage except, possibly, to the car that bumped him.

Do you remember reading of how the Bowery was 90 years ago? Of Kit Burns who would decapitate a live rat for 25 cents a bite; of Dandy Johnny Dolan who invented a copper device for use on the thumb for gouging out an opponent's eye? And of the toughest tough of all, Monk Eastman, whose price list for the Tammany politicians who hired him was:

| Ear Chewed Off | $15 |
| Leg or arm broken | $19 |
| Leg Shot | $25 |
| Stabbing | $25 |

Well, these were lovable rogues next to Evil.

You couldn't amass as much amorality as he had in a lifetime: it had to be built into the genetic structure somehow. It wasn't purely evil—it was bad evil. The worst kind.

There have doubtless been other humans as evil as he. Hitler comes to mind. But he was extenuated by a brain that occasionally reflected some cultural alertness, could paint a bit (I like his stuff better than Churchill's but the Britisher was a better bricklayer), and was a gravitating speaker.

Or take Jack the Ripper. In his off hours, this one could be downright congenial. More to the point, Jack used weapons; Evil never did—he was his own best weapon.

These types, then, at odd moments betrayed civilized attributes. Not so Evil. He never varied the basic pattern of his behavior which ran from sullen and chilling to the most volcanic violence and outrage. He was a hulking nightmare of a man.

He had a police record as long as a gorilla's arm and had been shot at least twice by outnumbered minions of the law coming athwart of him. The shots didn't take, however, and so he hied himself off always to new regions to indoctrinate the unsuspecting lawmen there in the true meaning of chaos.

Gerald Swanson, an ex-warden and thus one who should know, told me that Evil had served time in a California penal institution. He was released, believe it or not, for *bad behavior!* Really. He broke the jawbone of the first guard that tried to hurry him into a cell. I won't tell you what he did to the second offender—but that unlucky one was immediately pensioned off (at age 25) and is as sterile as Christianity today.

Not that he liked the prisoners any better. Rape is endemic in many prisons and it flourished there. But the first time five studs ganged up to try him he all but decapitated them, and almost drowned the leader in the toilet bowl. It took 14 guards and some excessive work with the billy clubs to pull him off the overwhelmed would-be rapists.

The state couldn't afford to continue giving him that much attention and through some legerdemain they put him back out on the street the first chance they got. After all, Swanson said, he hadn't actually killed anyone.

That was Evil and this was a Saturday night in Los Angeles; April, 1936. The place was alive with folks reaching for old dreams and new happiness. Evil walked in unremarked and unnoticed, a big guy, true, but there were always lots of big guys around. He walked with a sprawl, and though he didn't look steady or stable he walked straight ahead. People, sensing the awesome in him, got out of the way. He took a seat at the bar and ordered rye.

Charlie served him, quickly sizing him up as any good bartender will. But Evil was quiet and didn't throw out his chin when he talked, so Charlie put him in the "unknown" category. By their body language or voice some customers will let you know they're potential troublemakers; some will indicate that they're out for fun rather than frolic; but the other category, the "unknowns," don't give you enough to go on. So you watch the worst with both eyes, the "unknowns" with one.

Guys had come gunning for Charlie before. Charlie got so he could sense them. Most of them moseyed up, looked at his breadth and gaped at his fluid movement and kept going. The few who persisted were undone in various modes and sundered in sundry ways.

Evil sat there, saying not a word, and drank. An alive place got livelier. Jean Rule, a comely lass of 18 summers, came in at 10:30 and managed to get a place at the bar. She drank a coke and joshed with Charlie about her forthcoming marriage to Bill Jones, one of Charlie's regulars, who was working that night as a railway switchman. About 11 she turned to go but found her exit blocked. Unfortunately she had sat down next to Evil and, five ryes into the evening, he now had his big left mitt around her waist.

This has since struck me as curious, though it didn't then. I was in the middle of the bar talking to Charlie and didn't know Evil (I reconstructed what I knew of his life only later, after the fact), and would only have been surprised if an unattended girl could have gotten out the door without a play being made for her. Why it has puzzled me since is that Evil didn't fool with the girls. Sure, he'd get liquored up and if the moon was right he might end up with some poor wench, and he'd been known to demolish a whore-house on occasion, but the boy-girl thing, the charming coy inter-play before a pickup wasn't his glass of rye.

So why did he make a play for Jean? I believe that right from the start it wasn't Jean he was after. She was only bait for Charlie. He must have heard of Charlie's prowess time and again and it had festered in him—the fact that there was a big billy goat gruff somewhere who might give him some competition—so much that he'd hit town and come gunning for Charlie. He knew from the conversation between Jean and Charlie that he could provoke the big boy back of the bar by harrassing her.

Now I could lie and make this the epic struggle between good and evil that you expect. But I have to tell you the truth—what actually happened. So when I sidled out and saw the behemoth blocking Jean, I went on down toward the action. Near but not too near: I was a youngster and these guys were big.

When he saw what was happening, Charlie came around the bar and reached for Jean with his right hand and Evil snapped a hand around his wrist like the bite of a Doberman Pinscher. Charlie promptly compensated by grabbing Evil's left wrist. Each stood with a vise lock on one wrist of the other. Charlie's face had an amused expression on it; Evil's was consternation cooking. It was a Mexican standoff.

A strange and tense situation. Charlie was the bigger man, out-bulking Evil, but everyone seeing them close up in confrontation, was for Charlie. Evil exuded the negativism, the nihilism the world is better off without, and he had terrible eyes.

The Fomorian's champion, Balor (in Irish mythology) had one such eye, an orb so powerful it rendered antagonists helpless. Balor's eye opened only in warfare but Evil's whole life was war. Balor's eye was more powerful—it required four men just to raise the lid. (Lugh finally did the dread one in by slinging a boulder through the eye.) But, whereas Balor's eye was his only weapon, Evil's eyes—Charlie now in the furnace of their glare—were only one of many nefarious weapons he had about his person.

Evil's primeval mind couldn't cope with a draw. He let go of Charlie's wrists and Charlie released his. Evil was in a fair muddle at this point and very, very dangerous.

"You ____, ____, ____," he scooped out epithets like shovelfuls of gravel. "You sonofabitch, for that I now break up this place."

Charlie said cooly, "If you try, you got as much chance of success as a whore's prayer."

Just then the lights went out, all of them, outside as well as in. This wasn't unique in Los Angeles at that time: a new transformer had come on line at the local power authority and it had bugs in it, with the result that for several months that year a surge in usage would sometimes cause a power interruption.

First there were those grunts and cries of surprise which humans make when something really unexpected happens. But I wasn't interested in those. I heard some kind of movement from the two and then sensed something of high velocity coming toward me. I tried to step aside but the hurtling body caught me glancingly—fortunately—and the pair of us went back into the wall. I was younger then—and far shorter on ethics. As we rebounded from the wall, I assessed him quickly—it felt like Evil—measured him with a light left open hand on his shoulder, and then drove my right cross into what I hoped was his neck. I later learned it got him in the carotid artery. The body wavered and fell and I heard it sputter an epithet. Then I realized I had made a mistake: I had hit Charlie.

But I had put so much into the strike that I was unstable. The next thing I knew a cyclone brushed me and again I banged into the wall, the force passing me going a mile a minute, missing the recumbent Charlie, and smashing out through the large plate glass window into the street.

The next I knew, there was this terrible scream from out there. I couldn't figure it for a moment. Evil would never scream at pain—therefore, it couldn't be him.

But it was him—lying out there on the pavement as the lights all went on. He wasn't screaming at pain; he was screaming at death, writ large, coming at a gallop.

I got out there and knelt beside him and saw quick enough the why of the scream. I had once tended a man whose jugular had been severed in a car accident and I had been able to hold it together enough to prevent undue loss of blood until the rescue squad got there. But Evil had it worse. Shards of glass had opened his carotid and another artery in his right arm. The grim reaper was really slashing that night. The blood was gushing, not seeping, and a small crimson pool was already forming beside his body. Charon was paddling in it.

This was it. And he knew it. He then did an incredible thing. Through those glazed eyes he looked up at me and actually smiled. Then he died. You may conjecture that this first smile of his ugly life came when he realized that he was dying undefeated. But I think he welcomed death. He may have seen in death's grand satori that his bad karma had been expiated somehow; that somewhere there would be a new beginning where, perhaps, his long-dead soul could again function. If I am right, he lived more in that instant than he had in the 45 years of his life.

A pretty good ending then. Charlie ambled out, no worse for wear and tear, and looked at the corpse.

"Remember Dickens' line, "He'd make a lovely corpse," Johnny? One helluva fighter," he mused, "but he doesn't count."

"Why?" I asked.

"Because he lacked one thing the rest of us have. Humanity. This stiff is as alive now as he was ten minutes ago, humanly speaking. He was an animal or something worse. But he wasn't human."

I apologized to Charlie for mistaking him for Evil and knocking him down.

"Don't bother," he laughed, "you tagged me good. I was transfixed. But you probably did me a favor. If I had been left standing he would have hit me amidships. And if he had, who can say, the corpse on the pavement might have been someone else."

Martin Buber saw the evil in the world and agonized over it analytically. He ended by saying in effect: it's here and it can't be expunged. It can only be transformed.

Maybe he was right. Evil lying there was not so much dead as transformed. He had become good by dying. And maybe in his next reincarnation

*End of Evil*

he might even become tolerable.

So there you are. A story that doesn't particularly settle the ancient clash of good and evil. But it's a true one.

# VII

# SAVATE AND FRENCH BOXING

P. C. Wren in one of his delightful stories of the Foreign Legion wrote:

> At Ait-Ashsba, bad luck overtook Ramon Diego. At the *fon-*
> *dauk* he smote a burly Negro of Sokoto who jostled him. The Negro,
> one of a band of departing wayfarers, was a master of the art of
> *rabah*, the native version of *la savate*, and landed Ramon a most
> terrible kick beneath the breastbone. As he lay gasping and groaning
> for breath, the negro whipped out his razor-edged *yataghan* and
> bent over the prostrate man . . .

And we've all heard the story of a young beer-drinking Frenchman
seated on a stool in San Francisco tavern a few decades ago. Because he
looked "different" (the British would say " 'E's a stranger; 'eve 'alf a brick at
'im"), the Frenchman was approached and loudly insulted by a gargantuan
guy with shoulders so wide that he'd had to come into the tavern sideways.
The huge one was burning from the effects of whiskey. The Frenchman,
young in years with facial features all pink and white, minded not the
boisterous insults, until repetition reduced their niceties to mere cacophony.
This apparently hurt the artistic soul of the Frenchman for he swung around
on the stool to face his antagonist. Still holding a mug half-full of beer, he put
his other hand in his pocket.

The rough went into action instantly. He threw a right fist as big as a
small rosebush which would have demolished a shed, had it landed. Luckily
for our story, it did not. Coincident with the miss, the legs of the Frenchman
lashed out, the feet snapped up, and, quicker than the eye could follow, 10 or
more kicks hit the house that walked like a man. That worthy immediately
died for awhile. Then it was noticed that the youngster still sat atop the stool,
one hand in his pocket, and the other holding the beer mug still half full—not
a drop had spilled. The Frenchman spun back around to the bar and resumed
his drinking with some gusto.

This legend has gone around the globe and everyone retelling it swears he witnessed it at that San Francisco tavern. In a small midwestern town in 1943 I heard the story from two different persons. The frequency with which the story is told makes it appear that the encounter took place in a stadium rather than a tavern. However, the significant thing about the legend is that—like all legends—it is true. Somewhere, sometime, something like the legend happened, though its details have been embellished since.

Well, what is this "thing" we've been talking about. this French boxing? I gave an all-too-brief account of it in my discussion of the incomparable Baron Fegnier in my first book. Here I want to go into a good bit more detail.*

The great poet Theophile Gautier who lived during the zenith of French boxing's popularity said of it: "La Boxe Francaise is a profound science which requires much composure, calculation, and strength. It is the very best development of human vigor: a contest without arms in circumstances in which one should never be taken unawares."

French boxing doesn't have a long history. Nor was its origin lofty. It was born about 1830 from foot boxing, the sport of pimps and hoodlums, in which the guard was kept low, the hands in front and open. The low kick was about the only tactic: the chest or side kick wasn't known. These boxers were not able to employ a leg pickup and they used the hand only for slapping.** One such technique was the "coup de la musette" delivered

---

*My principal sources for this history are J. Charlemont's *La Boxe Francaise*, 1877; V. Casteres and Willie Lewis's *La Boxe: Traite Pratique et Complete*, 1908; J. Britt and J. Charlemont's *La Boxe Anglaise et Francaise*, 1911; P. Boucher's *La Boxe Francaise*, 1929; R. Poulain's *Sports de Combat*, 1946; Federatin Francaise de Boxe's *Statuts Reglements Interieurs Code Sportif*, 1957; L. Alliot and G. Prevot's *La Boxe Francaise*, no date; and a series by R. W. Smith published in the British journal *Judo* in the 1950's.

**James Thurber's article "A Sock on the Jaw-French Style" written for *Harper's Monthly Magazine* in 1924 made the point that the French argument never comes to blows. We know from some of Hemingway's expatriate friends that French law was harsh in respect to fisticuffs in the street. Malcolm Cowley was once arrested for fisticuffs in Paris and could have been jailed for six months. For the sake of accuracy let it be said that, Thurber's delightful essay and legal penalties notwithstanding, the mercurial French often went beyond the verbal in the street. But my research shows that where violence did ensue, the slap rather than the fist was the preferred mode.

with the base of the hand directly up into the nose of the opponent.

The originator and best fighter in this early style was Michel Pisseux. Born in Paris in 1794, he became a baker like his father. He was raised in the slums where fights were common and terror frequent. By watching fights, this gentle and quiet man was able to devise a system he called *savate* (old shoe). Pisseux's system derived from *chausson* (soft shoe) and *jeu Marseillais*. The *marsellais* method featured blows with the fist and higher kicks than *savate* but was deficient in that the adversaries seldom faced each other and most of the kicks missed due to a lack of space orientation.


"Before a serious systematic sport," Charlemont says in his splendid text, "the Marseillais school could not hold up; it is, if one wishes, for gymnastics, for dance, for clowning, but it is not for combat and for defense."

We don't know for sure, of course, but insofar as *savate* seems to have gone from Marseilles to the Paris underworld in the first two decades of the nineteenth century, one can speculate that its rudiments came from Chinese sailors putting in at the southern port.

But back to Michel Pisseux. He never provoked a fight; indeed, it is said he fought only if his back was against the wall. After teaching a while he was able to quit the slums for more fashionable surroundings. Famous people came to him for instruction, the best known being the Duke of Orleans and Lord Seymour.

One writer of the period sketched this picture of Pisseux, the terror of la Courtille. "He was 36 with a dull face marked by smallpox; his grey eyes were wily; his limbs long and bony; his big hands had knotty fingers with the toughness of wood. His rapid and disjointed gestures recalled a man sending semaphore signals. He wore a short jacket and roomy trousers of brown cloth, and a cap with an enormous tassel."

After his years of triumph, Pisseux went into a long decline, dying in abject poverty at 75, forgotten by his own generation and almost unknown to the new.

Early foot boxing was learned in the streets. But as men of fashion began to seek instruction, gyms cropped up. Pisseux's best student, Charles Lecour, began teaching in 1830 at the age of 24. Lecour had spent eight years under Pisseux, but even when he had reached the apex he was dissatisfied: he realized that the French style over-emphasized use of the feet whereas the British put too much stress on the hands. In consequence, both were half arts. Wanting to blend the best of the two, he went to England and, disguised as a novice, he took instruction in the British style from Swift and Adams, two of the best boxers in London.* Satisfied with his proficiency in this sport, he returned to France. By synthesizing the two styles, *savate* and British boxing, he created French Boxing.

Lecour had a tremendous success. Aristocrats from all quarters of France flocked to him for instruction. He gave lessons to Eugene Sue, author of the novel, *Les Mysteres de Paris,* who had him fictionally teach the art to his main character, Prince Rodolphe.**

The palmy period of French boxing was the decade 1845-1855 when public matches were conducted at the Cirque Olympique by Charles and Hubert Lecour and at the Montesquieu salon by Leboucher (see below). Hubert Lecour was a fascinating fighter: rather short, he was equally adept with fist and foot, especially at close quarters. His counters were so rapid the eye could not follow. Of Charles, one reporter wrote: "Charles Lecour had lifted *savate* up to the dignity of English boxing. His methods are excellent because they work all parts of the body. With this means of defense, a man can leave his cane or revolver at home."

Shortly after the Lecours opened their gym, two provincial teachers— Loze of Toulose and Leboucher of Rouen—arrived in Paris. Loze's technique was similar to Lecour's but Leboucher, a great master of the cane, had legs too short for greatness. Though he seldom fought in public, he was an excellent teacher and turned out fine boxers. These three men gave superiority to the Paris school, making the crude Marseillais art from the south, the unscientific mauling, look poor by comparison.

Leboucher, born in 1807, besides being a master of cane and stick

---

*The source for this is Charlemont, but it may be too romantic to be true. In another place, Charlemont states that Lecour and Loze fought the Englishman, Oliver Swift, at the home of Lord Seymour and were thoroughly beaten. Later, Lecour watched a fight between Swift and Adams, another leading British boxer, and saw that his style had to be modified. After taking a series of lessons from Adams, who had remained for a while in Paris, he meshed the fist and foot into French Boxing.

**Rodolphe ran up against a convict skilled in *savate* in the very first chapter. The convict quickly learned a lesson. The slender slight individual in the dark Paris street tossed the big fellow twice and then rained on him "a shower of blows with his closed fist, as hard and heavy as if struck by a steel gauntlet. These blows, worthy of the admiration of Jem Belcher, Dutch Sam, Tom Cribb, or any other celebrated English pugilist, were so entirely different from the system of the *savate,* that the Chourineur dropped like an ox on the pavement, exclaiming, as he fell, 'I'm floored!'"

fighting, was the first boxer to bring the knockout to the fore. He encouraged his students to go into the streets and match up with the tough 'uns there. He would say to them when they came into the gym: "Well, children, you'll never amount to anything!" One of the methods Leboucher introduced—so extreme that it was barred in public fights—was the direct kick with the toe of the foot.

Although rough and a good wrestler, Leboucher was too short and never appeared in public bouts. But this didn't negate his value in teaching fierce techniques. He loved to drink and, in his cups, was a danger to all who had the misfortune to be in the gym at that time. Because of this, many gave up their lessons despite having paid in advance. He came a cropper one night when one of his pupils, Coeurderoi, gave him such a beating that he refused to teach him any longer, saying that he didn't want to have anything further to do with such a brute! The famous artist Daumier caught the rough aspect of Leboucher in a cartoon titled "A Boxing Lesson with Leboucher."

If he had limitations as a boxer, Leboucher had none as a promoter. The boxing, fencing, cane, and wrestling displays he put on at the Montesquieu, Valentino, Redoute, Casino de Arts, and Markowski's were very successful. He discovered and launched Arpin (called the Savoyard) and promoted other wrestlers such as Rabasson, Crest (the Bull from Provence), Rivoire (the Man Made of Marble), Pujol (the Bridge-pile), Marseilles the Elder (the first man to beat Arpin), and later, Etienne (the Shepherd), Richous, and others. By his efforts, wrestling in France was roused from its apathy.

And of course he put on splendid boxing displays featuring Rambaud, Vigneron, Bernard, and others. Perhaps the most brilliant was a match at the Casino des Arts in 1850 pitting Rambaud (called "The Resistance") against Bernard, the most famous boxer/wrestler in southern France. They fought with great vigor, and equally, until Rambaud brought his opponent down with a resounding kick in the chest. The audience, shocked by the sudden end, applauded long and loud. Three years later another important match placed Rambaud against Arpin. The latter had been defeated for the first time at wrestling the year before by Marseilles the Elder and was out to redeem himself. Rambaud, however, was far superior and thoroughly defeated him.

Rambaud was the favorite of the crowds until displaced by Vigneron. A baker by profession, he was big, powerful, and one of the few men to excel in boxing, wrestling, the cane, and weightlifting. Though he was large, well-proportioned, and intelligent, Rambaud lacked the ability to be a good demonstrator. But he was tough in real matches and also turned out first-rate products, the weightlifter Henri Joignerey being one of his proteges.

Later in life he fell on bad days. Coeurderoi saw him in Switzerland in 1876.

No longer young, his body had been marked by life and was puffed up. He had done so many things! Back from the Middle East where the Egyptian Redive, Ismail Pasha, had told him "Blessed be the bosom of the mother who carried you," he had wrestled in Greece. He spent two years drinking, eating, and hunting, but stopped this when his funds were exhausted. When I met him at the station, he was dressed as a sailor and was exhibiting a stuffed fish he billed as a "shark."

Later, Charlemont met him in Antwerp where Rambaud had a stand at a fair. It was difficult to recognize the splendid athlete of yesteryear.

Other fighters of note during this period were Curel, the monkey-like southerner; the cold emotionless Tessier; Ducros; Rambaud, and the peerless Vigneron. Charles Ducros was a painting contractor by day, a boxing teacher at night. He fought in public using the British style—he alone was able to specialize in it, so much so, in fact that he beat the celebrated Cribb. Once in a match with the giant Vigneron he scored to the head. Vigneron pretended that he wasn't touched. "You were touched," Leboucher who was refereeing said. "You," expostulated Vigneron, "I return 18 or 20 to you." "I know well," countered Leboucher with a voice like an enchanting bell, "because you have great legs." Ducros and Vigneron finished by embracing to the cheers of the crowd.

The greatest boxer of all was Louis Vigneron. Born in 1827 to a carpenter who had served under Napoleon I in Spain and educated as an engineer, Vigneron left that profession when he was 21 because of weak eyes. He turned then to teaching boxing which he had studied for some time with Guerineau. He quickly became famous and even his father, who had opposed his decision to move into this field, applauded him. Once in a tavern a friend had tried to tackle him and Vigneron threw him over his head out an open window, unfortunately killing him. As this was done in play, the victim's family bore him no grudge. In fact he became engaged to a sister of the deceased, but she died of tuberculosis before the wedding.

About 1850 Vigneron's fame spread when Leboucher came to his gym and asked him to meet Rambaud. This one was the idol of the populace: tall, handsome, powerful. They fought three times at one week intervals; the first two were draws and the last was won by Vigneron's powerful feet.

Charlemont wrote that Vigneron was the most dangerous fighter ever

*Louis Vigneron, the Greatest Savate Master*

known, a "couilles de bronze" (man of great courage). Because of his great
size and tremendous strength, he stood far above the next best. He seemed
slower than Lecour, Ducros, and Charlemont but this was offset by his
power. Because of his unusual strength he was forced to restrain his kicks,
giving the impression of slowness.

In 1852 he was challenged by Arpin, at that time king of the wrestlers—a
good test of his strength. Alas, Arpin was no match for him. When the fight
began he jumped about and made foolish attacks but was stopped at every
turn by Vigneron's kicks. Several times Vigneron matched him at grappling
and threw him out of the ring. When the debacle ended Arpin's girl friend hid
near Vigneron's dressing room and attacked him with a sabre which he easily
deflected.

In 1854 Leboucher set up a fight for Vigneron with Dickson, the famous
British fighter, one which would establish the superiority of the two styles of
boxing. In the dressing room before the fight Dickson sneered at Vigneron
and stripped, displaying a magnificent physique. In English he told a friend
that Vigneron would not last three minutes with him. This was translated to
Vigneron who became upset. But when he stripped, Dickson's smile left
his face.

In the ring the two were about the same age and weight; both were cold as
ice at the start. Dickson extended his fists and kept his legs straight. Vigneron
lightly danced about; Dickson surveyed him, retreated, but left an opening.
Vigneron's foot landed on his jaw. At this, Dickson attempted to rush his
antagonist but Vigneron kept him at bay with his lashing feet. A foot in the
stomach caused Dickson's knees to sag. Vigneron now was the complete
master, smiling and skipping about the ring. The fight ended when Vigneron
fetched up a smart kick that landed behind Dickson's neck and caused the
Britisher to fall backwards only to be caught and held up by Vigneron.*

Vigneron also was a top weightlifter but his circus stunts in this realm
eroded his boxing prestige with the public. He once proposed to carry a live
bull on his back around the ring at the Hippodrome but never did, presuma-
bly because he couldn't get what he regarded as a sufficient fee to do it.
Although he was a showman, he was also hell in the street. He was set upon
once by eight hoods armed with knives. He knocked four of them down with

---

*Rambaud later met the Englishman and with some dirty tactics dislocated his
arm. Thereupon Vigneron jumped into the ring, chastised Rambaud for his tactics,
and challenged him on the spot. Rambaud, shocked to see a Frenchman—and such a
Frenchman—take the side of the Britisher, refused the challenge.

his cane and the other four fled from the area.

The stunts ended up undoing Vigneron. He was called "The Human Canon" because of his ability to hold a 440 pound cannon on his shoulders and fire it. The end doesn't come until it does, and on August 22, 1871, Vigneron tried the trick once too often; the discharge shattered his kidneys.

The matches Leboucher sponsored at the Montesquieu were the rage of Paris. The English boxer Cribb, who had settled in Paris, appeared there several times. Wrestling was also first-rate until Marseilles the Elder "spoiled it by introducing the knockout" [this quote from Joseph Charlemont probably refers to the practice of show (fake) wrestling]. In 1856 the police prohibited public matches. Then the Montesquieu became a restaurant and thereafter French Boxing was relegated to the gyms except for an occasional show put on by Vigneron and Lecour (done as benefits and thus acceptable to the police). But the zest had gone out of it and neither Vigneron nor Lecour could get good challengers. By 1862, French Boxing as a public spectacle was dead.

Just at this time a new star flashed across the sky. As Vigneron was preparing a show, he was visited by a young soldier named Joseph Charlemont who wanted to fight in it. The big one threw him some gloves, said: "Let's see what you can do."

After a few passes, Vigneron said, "That will do, but you must come and practice with me every day."

Charlemont asked, "And will I box at your match?"

"Yes."

"With whom?"

Vigneron paused, then said with emphasis, "With me."

In the match, the unschooled Charlemont was brilliant but still lacked the technique to compete with Vigneron, who carried him. After a year this powerful youngster with the catapult legs had progressed so much that Vigneron really had to work to defeat him. But always the differences in body size favored the bigger man.

People wondered how the newcomer would fare against the great Hubert Lecour, so a dream match was arranged in 1866. Because Charlemont had trained with the slower Vigneron, the betting favored Lecour. And at first, when he took three successive low leg kicks, the odds seemed correct. But Charlemont didn't lose his cool; steadied, and by the end of the hour was able to win the decision.

This established Charlemont's reputation. After organizing boxing and cane work in many regiments, he retired from the army, opened a gym in Paris, but also taught in Brussels. During this period he also defeated an

English boxer in a match to establish the supremacy of one of the two systems. "Charlemont was victorious, but with great pain; without batting an eye, the Englishman took terrific low kicks without even trying to avoid them," wrote a historian, Dr. Peugniez.

Shortly after the Franco-Prussian War, Hubert Lecour died and Raynal took over his gym; Rive followed Vigneron; Chauderlot, a sparring partner of Charlemont, accepted pupils; and Charles Lecour came out of retirement.

Charlemont's son, Charles, and another leading student, Casteres, in 1893 established the Academy of French Boxing and the Cane in Paris and ten years later the Federation of French Boxing was chartered. This gym, along with others run by Mainquet, Bayle, Chabrier, the LeClerc brothers, and Quillier were the chief places of instruction through 1914 in Paris. During this period the Desruilles brothers (Lille and Roubaix), Allart (Marseilles), and Boucher (Amiens) pushed the art in the provinces.*

Because professors had to pull their punches in teaching, it ruined them as professionals. In a boxing journal which noted the annual exhibition given by Charlemont's gym, we read:

French Boxing is appreciated but something is lacking to attract youngsters to this wonderful sport. Nowadays, the public wants to see a real fight, not an exhibition—even by masters. Exhibitions by masters are useful but real fights must be organized to show the remarkable tool French Boxing is for defense.

World War I ended further evolution. Many boxers were involved and some, including Maurice Casteres, son of the famed Professor, and Hubert Desruilles, were casualties. At the end of the war French Boxing lost its primacy to English boxing which drew larger audiences and greater purses. It never regained its stature. From 1918 through 1939 many gyms closed, the only noteworthy ones remaining open being those of Charlemont, Prevot, Surenois, Bouchez (Amiens), Grumelart (Boulogne-sur-Mer), Allart (Marseilles), and one in Lyon. Charlemont died in 1941 and the art with him. Following World War II the dwindling art lost out, this time to judo.

---

*Other noteworthies of this period were Rouy, Brost, Toutard, Caen, Baptiste, and Sabatier. At about this time one Petit, a boxer and fencer, went to New Orleans where he had many adventures. He became a success as a teacher there by killing in a sabre duel an accomplished duellist. Unfortunately, I have been unable to find out more on this worthy.

Its last luminary was Count P. Baruzy and even its name was changed to Parisian French Boxing. The form tried to merge with judo. Jean Beaujean, the celebrated judo expert, wrote of it: "French boxing is so very like judo, it is a pity it is dying out. But a merger of the two will give it new life and will result in a perfect self defense."

French boxing did not merge with judo. But since the mid-1960's karate has stimulated its resurgence.* The government has helped by establishing a separate section for it in the French Federation of Judo and Associated Arts. While participation probably has not caught up with the 100,000 total that practiced French boxing at the turn of the century, it is growing steadily. There is even cross-training occurring between its schools and those of karate. And the cane is again finding favor by being included in the curriculum. Currently, there are at least four major matches each year through which students can move through a series of colored gloves—not belts. Rank progression goes this way:

| Color of Gloves | Rank |
|---|---|
| blue | beginner |
| green | one year's training |
| chestnut | contest participant |
| red | championships participant |
| silver | instructor |
| gold | professor |

The rules have changed somewhat. Wrestling is now barred, draws are acceptable, and you can use only two successive punches before you must pause or use a kick.

In the regulations of 1911, there were eight weight categories. Four things were barred:

- direct kicks with the toe or ball of foot

- hitting the opponent's head in chancery

- slapping and hitting with wrist, elbow, knee, or head

- striking between the groin and the navel

---

*In fact, a recent champion has travelled to Japan, reportedly demolishing all the karate competition there.

The rules called for three three-minute rounds, with one-minute rests, and, if a draw, the referee would allow a fourth round. There could be no draws in the extension. The first man to score four points in the fourth round won the match. Points were awarded as follows:

| Technique | Points |
|---|---|
| block | 1 |
| low kick | 2 |
| body kick | 3 |
| face kick | 4 |
| leg pick-up | 2 |
| leg pick-up and throw | 4 |

Punches to the body and head counted the same as kicks. If a man didn't heed the referee's call to "stop" he was assessed four points. And if a boxer stalled for more than ten seconds, he could be disqualified. A boxer knocked down had to get up by the count of ten or lose the match.

The rules obtaining in 1877 encouraged more wrestling (if a boxer failed to get out of a hold after several seconds, he was penalized) and discouraged sequence strikes (the fighter himself announced the blow he was struck with). The point system, too, was slightly different, but overall the rules were pretty much the same as in the 1911 set.

In the 1950's R. W. Smith did a brief critique of French Boxing which, based as it was on Charlemont's *La Boxe Francaise, Traite Theorique et Pratique,* is generally sound. I reproduce some of it (with his permission) below.

"Charlemont believed that a boxer must have four qualities, *viz.,* the ability to anticipate, composure, agility, and adroitness. The first two are innate but the latter two can be acquired only by practice. In a match the boxers wear regulation boxing gloves, which were much lighter earlier, and cloth shoes. Basically there are two guard positions, right and left, not at all dissimilar from aikido and karate postures. I will describe in some detail the left guard posture. The reader will realize that the right guard posture is the same position led by the right, rather than the left, side of the body. To assume the left guard, take your right foot about 18 inches to the rear. Execute a half turn to the right. The toes of your left foot should now be directed toward your opponent, and those of your right foot to your right. Your heels should be on the same line. Your left leg should be straight without stiffness and your right leg slightly bent. Your weight rests largely on the rear foot (at least a 60-40 ratio in favor of the rear foot).

"Your body is held erect and your eyes should look directly at the opponent. Your left arm in front is half bent, the left fist at chin level, nails turned toward your face. Your right arm has its elbow at the body, the closed fist level with your left breast and slightly apart from the body. Your fingernails should be turned toward your chest and your right shoulder thrown back slightly.

"From these positions eight principal blows with the hands or feet are delivered in the form of leads, combinations, feints, or counters. Space orientation is important. A proficient boxer is able to ascertain to the nearest inch the distance which separates him from his adversary. As in judo, the spectacular trick seldom is the most rational. The more serious foot blows are those not going higher than the chest. The sensational high foot blows are dangerous for, if they miss, the user's center of gravity is displaced, surrendering him to the counter of his opponent.

"One major weakness of French boxing is a functional one concerned with the basic guards. No provision is made for a person 'off guard.' Both boxers must have the same guard. If one is standing in right guard and the other left guard, they are considered 'wrongly on guard.' To extend this to a street situation, if a man in right guard attacks you while you are in left guard you may be in difficulty since you haven't been trained fighting in mixed positions. On this score aikido and karate are a good deal more functional.

"One of the leaders in French judo circles wrote me nearly a decade ago that French boxing was superior, in his mind, to karate. Since then, he has become one of the leaders in the importation of karate into France and, learning more about karate, he has, I believe—though tact forbids my asking—revised his opinion. In my study of both, I give the palm to karate. Karate is superior in that attacking members are hardened; more members are used (the elbow, knee, etc.,); and movements are less circular and use the entire body, not merely a leg or arm divorced from body weight. In short, I think that the mechanism of the body is more efficient, powerful, and swift in karate than in French boxing.

"This is not to minimize the latter, however. 'Boxing with Four Limbs' is the best method of self defense to come from Europe. Men like the Lecours, Vigneron, and the Charlemonts were of the same substance as the judo leaders of the Kodokan at the turn of the century."

To criticize the critique, Smith may be incorrect on false guard. Boxers had to know how to fight from this position and questions were always asked about it on the teacher certification examinations. Moreover, strikes were never pulled.

Smith says that aikido and karate are more functional. After all this time I'm sure he would change his judgment on this. Functionally, aiki just is not a proven article. Even in practice, it has too many moves before a result is achieved. Karate *in theory* is as he describes it—a total body response but, again, it has yet to be translated to street use.* As Funakoshi himself warned, it must have utility or it remains a dance. The question is moot, finally. But if I had to choose between Vigneron and Oyama to slum with in gay old Paree, I'd opt for the Frenchman.

Now let me expand the discussion. Dr. Rouhet, a student of Chauderlot, writes:

> In a few words, this is the theory of French Boxing as it was established by Charlemont and Chauderlot: on one stretched leg used as a support, fixed and immobile, the boxer hits with the foot of the other leg. The kick must be violent, sharp, and precise. The balance must not be lost. Of course it is rather difficult to obtain such a result and that is what makes French Boxing less attractive and more difficult to learn. An individual who trains in French Boxing has to train his whole body, the upper as well as the lower part.

Rouhet believed that 5'8" tall was the ideal height for French boxing. If too short, one had trouble reaching the opponent; if too tall, one was apt to be too slow. Most great boxers were taller than 5'8" and were very durable. But physiques varied. Chauderlot was tall and thin; Raynal, thick-set but vigorous. Body position was built on fencing. French boxing was similar to t'ai-chi in that weight was kept pretty much on one leg; but dissimilar in that the stance was narrower. Full torso power was unavailable because the feet made a narrower base than the shoulders.

Perhaps the greatest difficulty is in this body position: it must be kept balanced so that the muscles of the thigh and leg which kick can contract easily and quickly without loss of balance.

While French boxing may have got less of the body into the kick, the fighter seldom lost balance as a result of the kick as do many *karateka*.

---

*In fact, the highly graded Frenchman Smith mentioned, a mutual friend, never changed his mind. He found that French boxing easily prevailed over karate. He used graded Japanese black belts and was somewhat disappointed because he was promoting karate at the time. The biggest difficulty was in getting the Japanese to admit that karate was not yet a total system. There was too much dogmatism and arrogance for them to modify what they had learned.

Moreover, in the French style the body was much more supple and relaxed than in karate. Both types fail lamentably as regards use of the arms and fists. I have seen Baruzy and others and it is clear that they have given the field over to the foot so completely, that the hands are forgotten. From this standpoint both are far inferior to western boxing in practice. Of course, western boxing cannot approach them in total use of the body because it bars leg attacks.

Guillemin, former world champion in the art, in writing of how Anglo-American boxing supplanted the French style, puts much of the onus on the knockout punch of the former, saying it was almost non-existent in the latter. This was because of the priority afforded the feet and the fact that high kicks just were not that effective in a contact match (*karateka* please note). In Anglo-American boxing the knockout was largely a function of fists that could go to the head safely without destroying one's own balance. The knockout itself was not common until Anglo-American boxing rules were amended so that a man was permitted only ten instead of thirty seconds to rise from the mat.

Knockouts are rare because most kicks are kept low. The low kick is used for attack and countering. In it you try to reach the inside of the opponent's tibia where the skin is thin and touches the bone which can be broken fairly easily. Here's how it's done. Take a left guard. Flex your left leg slightly and throw back your upper torso as you swing your right foot, stretched along the thigh, skimming along the ground by the shortest direct route to the inside of his right tibia. Your right toes are outward and you strike with the inner aspect of the foot. The strike, note, is against the inner tibia of his right leg. To effectuate this, he must be standing in a false guard: that is, his right foot forward is opposed to your left foot forward. The technique won't work against his left foot which your right foot would have to strike on the outside of the tibia, where it is protected by numerous muscles. If your opponent is leaning forward, the strike may fracture the tibia. If is for this reason that the weight is always carried on the rear leg in French boxing.

The low kick is supplemented by flank kicks going to the sides or pit of the stomach, cross kicks, and hopping kicks, the toe or heel being used as the situation and personal technique dictates. Kicks to the face, as mentioned above, are rarely used because of the problem of balance. Parries, blocks, and counters are adapted to all the kicks and the fists are blended in as both attacking and defending members.

How practical is French boxing? In theory, because it combines striking by the four appendages, it should be great in the street. But as with most systems it really comes down to how well the individual can use his wares, and —in French boxing, particularly—his feet. The side kick aims between the thorax and the pelvis, but only the real experts can deliver it higher with safety. The direct kick (banned in regulated matches) aims at the scrotum or stomach with the tip of the foot while the upper body sharply retracts. The new rules banning wrestling, however, really do it a disservice for street use. For there, grappling as well as striking is a prerequisite to success. The great boxers of old were, like Peter Maher and John L. Sullivan, accomplished wrestlers. The new crop has to depend on more fluency in the hands and legs to overcome this deficiency.

# VIII

# A KAHUNA CONQUERS TEXAS

*You may like t' work t' system,*
*All yore moves laid out in text,*
*But yuh lose a heap of livin'*
*Wen yuh know jus' what comes next."*
—J. R. Williams

The U.S. currently has two energy problems. One is to get sufficient fuel to power our economy. The other is the search by many for esoteric energy and skills with which to change their lives and remake the world. These skills can be gotten in a variety of ways, but what Americans don't seem to understand is that in the highest occult schools the discipline is done for its own sake, not for the secret powers that sometimes come. The powers are simply an offshoot of the discipline. And these skills, though they may seem supernormal, actually are regarded as impediments to spiritual growth.

I met Baron Eugene Fersen several times and I saw him do some extraordinary things. But what impressed me most about him was how he derided these "tricks," even though he was authentically doing things that the Israeli magician, Uri Geller, only pretends to do. Fersen felt that rationality was coming back to the world, and, along with Teilhard de Chardin, that civilization was on its way up to the Omega Point. I'm a bit more pessimistic. Nothing I see around me makes me lean toward their roseate view.

Anyhow, Fersen believed that on the way up we should all see more and more of the manifestations of the *avatars* (living Gods) among us. But he would say, "Watch the *avatars* and not their tricks."

I've always believed that Fersen, though a European, got most of his ability from his work in the ancient Hawaiian art of Lua. This most secret method of the Kahuna warriors is about the only thing that can explain Fersen's ability in magnetism, knocking a man down from a distance, and so on. There are many stories about Lua, a world of which James Michener is totally unaware.

The magic of Lua was handed down by Kahunas (Keepers of the Secret). These experts could walk on fire, read and send thoughts, cure cancer, and harness the vital force *(mana)* to such an extent that some could "wish" an enemy to death. Small wonder that the Hawaiian authorities barred its practice.

Lua was a secret art never performed publicly and didn't even get into a Hawaiian dictionary until 1865 when it was defined as "bonebreaking... and much practiced in ancient times." The dictionary was right about its history. It was practiced in the 1700's and by 1790 was at its peak. But it has been dying ever since. In this century, H. Okazaki, who brought jujutsu to Hawaii, once told me that Lua was far better than his stuff. (Another researcher, Charles Kenn, had some material describing its moves but must have been under a vow because he wouldn't share it.)

I was able to learn something after a lot of digging. The dictionary had been incomplete on its definition. Lua contained much more than mere bonebreaking. It had features resembling ju-jutsu, judo, and aikido as well as the inner arts *(nei-chia)* of Chinese boxing. These latter were in the realm of nerve attacks, knocking down from a distance, and other esoterica. Indeed, Lua was a catalog of nefarious skills. It was a much higher, more sophisticated thing than the *mokomo,* the hard barefisted fighting that Captain Cook saw on his Hawaiian trips in the eighteenth century.

One of the strangest stories I have heard on this ancient Polynesian magic concerned an obscure army dogface with the unlikely name of Carl Sawyer. His name struck me as odd because he was a full-blown original-vintage Hawaiian, but he had been orphaned early by a car accident, and adopted by an American professor and his wife living on Oahu.

Sawyer never let on to his own people that he practiced Lua or that he was a Kahuna, a high priest. His natural father gave him the blood; his uncle, the secret teachings. His friends and neighbors never knew. But I did. His actions in one incident gave away the game to anyone who, like myself, was versed in the work of Max Freedom Long.

I got news of this second-hand. Al Laney told me. He had witnessed the thing—it had awed him awfully—and he narrated it to me. But because Al knew nothing of Lua he really didn't know the implications of what he had seen. But I knew. Let me simply paraphrase Al and fill in the gaps.

Carl Sawyer was a company clerk in an Army unit training in Texas during World War II. He was short, slender, and unnoticed. The original Mr. Anonymous, he bothered no one and no one noticed him enough to bother him.

The tedium of that kind of sandy, raw life meant that everyone sooner or later targeted in on someone else. You vented the frustration caused you by the Axis powers onto some guy who had nothing to do with the abnormal life you were living. Such a life cried out for bruised knuckles and split lips.

So a lot of head-banging went on. In fact, out of 100 or so men in the company only five were immune to this rite. There was Stu Warren, the 6 foot 5-ish ex-Police Lieutenant from L.A. who only spoke by grunt and only grunted in expletives. And there was Jesse Curtis from the 'Bama cotton fields, not as big as Stu, but as the Golden Gloves open heavy champ in Mobile in 1939, figured to be about as tough.

The third one exempt was Al Laney, my source. Al was a clowning laughing devil of a guy who had been undefeated as an amateur boxer and had won his first six pro goes on K.O.'s before the war changed all that. Although only a middleweight, Al had never lost outside the ring either. He and Stu and Jesse weren't friends but there was too much cautionary respect for them to be enemies. Like three pretty girls in high school, their relationship was cool but impeccable.

The fourth fellow was Carl but, as I said above, he had that status because he was zilch, a cipher, not worth the slight effort it would take to squash him verbally or physically.

The fifth and foremost exempt from violence was Bull Masters, the company top sergeant. No one picked on him simply because nearly everyone was scared to death of him. Bull wasn't more than 5'10" but he looked, terrifyingly, the same size sidewise. His 260 pounds wasn't all that hard—it sloshed a bit when he walked—but he was hell in the street.

He was that strange hybrid synthesized from the south in the century since it lost the Civil War. This is a form of human being compounded of ignorance, fundamentalist churchianity, violence against the weak, unbending loyalty to a superior, and the amorality of a weasel. This character type did an awful lot of the dirty work following along in the good war (World War II) and leading in the bad war (Vietnam).

You don't expect this type to befriend the orphan, visit the sick, or solace the sorrowful. That's what some chaplains are for. But you do expect a first sergeant to have some rapport with his troops. Not Bull. He was a perfect bureaucrat—he didn't want rapport, he wanted fear. He never said a civil word to anyone in the company and a couple of weeks after joining the outfit, when he'd sized the boys up, separating them from the men, he began systematically to work his way through the troops.

It was work he understood and loved. He would elicit a slow or—worse—curt response to an order by one of the men. He would then put his nose against the offender and proceed to read him off royally. This was the crucial time in the process: if the miscreant resisted this verbal violence, Bull would offer to go out back, take off his stripes, and have it out. It was an offer few accepted. Most of them took it, feeling shame, but feeling fear more.

In such a situation the sadist usually will exempt the more powerful. But give Bull this—no one was immune to his tune. He played and everyone had to dance. So by the time he'd worked his way through to a face-off with the tough ones—Stu, Jesse, and Al—he was as avid for it as Chesterton said children used to be for butterscotch.

Bull began on the street elite by bracing Al Laney. Al took the verbal, but when Bull physically pushed him a bit, Al shoved back. Well, they went out back, Bull smiling and Al sober. Less than five minutes later Bull was smiling more obscenely when he returned to the formation to announce to the troops that he had had a good lunch, and had just disposed of one troublemaker, did anyone else want to give it a go? No one stepped forward—but Stu and Jesse were thinking deep thoughts: they knew their times were coming.

Al told me that he and Bull hadn't had a fight; they had had a war. Al found Bull easy to hit—too easy. At first Al thought it was going to be a cakewalk. He hit him with his best shots but the only one it bothered was Al. Bothered? It scared the hell out of him. Those shots which had upended so many lesser mortals didn't faze Bull at all. His armor was undented. When the daunted Al got in close Bull simply manhandled him, turning him every which way but loose. "He was the toughest hombre I ever met," Al sighed ruefully in recalling the event for me. "Afterwards," he said, "I felt like the Irishman who, asked how he felt after a fracas, says 'Like ten men, seven dead and three in the hospital.'"

Well, a subdued Al marshalled his aches and bruises and rejoined the ranks. And he told Stu and Jesse about it, laying it on the line. If Stu and Jesse had been confident before about giving Bull his come-uppance when their turns came, their confidence sagged a mite. And after mulling it for a while, Stu suggested that the three of them gang up on Bull. The primeval beast probably would accept. But when Al said he wouldn't even take those odds, Stu and Jesse's remaining confidence fled, and by the time Bull got to them they were almost completely psyched out.

To tell it terse, Jesse lasted five minutes and Stu, seven, with the monster. Stu went into the hospital. Al talked to him later and Stu told him that things were going OK until he kneed Bull twice in the groin, and Bull put his hands out, waved them invitingly, and said: "The third strike's on me." Then Stu died inside, packed it in, and shuffled off shortly afterwards to dreamsville.

With these warriors out of the way, Bull got restive. Like Alexander the

Great as a child complaining to his father that he had left him no one to conquer, Bull looked around, frustrated. But there was no one else. Except, that is, the modest heretofore unscathed company clerk, Carl Sawyer. So Bull started in on him. But there wasn't too much fun in it. Carl took every insult placidly and continued to do his clerical work. Bull would call him a fool and Carl would smile and go on typing. This made Bull madder than ever. Besides, there was no one left to pick on. So Bull kept needling and Carl took it servilely, anxious not to give offense.

It reminded me of Epictetus, the father of Stoic philosophy, who was a slave of a sadistic Roman Emperor. One day, the bored Emperor was twisting Epictetus' leg. "Might I observe, your highness," Epictetus said calmly, "that you are twisting my leg beyond its limits and if you persist it will break." The emperor went on twisting and there was the inevitable crack. At which Epictetus observed: "Your highness, you will recall that I told you earlier that if you persisted in twisting my leg it would break. You did and it has!"

Bull put cornflakes in Carl's bunk and short-sheeted him, put shaving cream in his boots, and such nefarious little things. Carl would laugh quietly like he had deserved it and go back to work.

The thing that brought it all to a head was Carl's penchant for beer. Now, he didn't drink much, just one can a day in fact. But it meant a lot to him and he drank it almost as if it were sacramental wine. He'd examine the can, nursing it round with his thin fingers, open it, and savor its taste, nursing it along for 20 minutes or so. During this ritual he never spoke. And almost no one noticed it at the time; Laney recalled it only in hindsight.

But Bull, frustrated at not getting a rise out of Carl, may have finally lit on it. Or perhaps he found this chink in Carl's armor only by chance. Regardless, whether it was by design or accident, Bull finally got a reaction from the little clerk one night at the battalion enlisted bar. When Carl went to the toilet, Bull pissed in his beer.

Carl came sauntering docile as a calf back to the slaughter. He picked up his can, eyed it lovingly, and took a drink. He set the can down abruptly as the place exploded with laughter. But this didn't seem to faze him: he just sat there, betrayed by the sacrilege, looking at the can.

Bull roared with laughter, "I added some vitamins for you, keed; how'd they go down?"

Carl looked up at him with a vacant look, smiled ruefully, said: "Fine, just fine. One swig was enough though. But say, Sarge, I've got to type up that order on uniforms I told you about this afternoon, and I need your help on it. Could you drop by the company tent later?"

Bull had had his triumph and beamed on Carl. "Sure, I'll drop over after

*Bull and the Beer Additive*

another beer."

Carl left then, the fellows still laughing. About ten minutes later Bull left. Laney, sensing something, tagged along a couple of minutes later. By the time he got down to the company tent, Bull had already gone in and the front flap was closed. Al lingered outside. He heard voices, Bull's strident, Carl's soft. Then a noise, more noise, a helluva commotion. Then an eerie sound unlike anything Al had ever heard before. It wasn't a scream but it screamed of extremity, loss, death. Al feared for Carl, but the memory of his own beating kept him rooted where he stood.

Then the damnedest thing happened. Carl Sawyer opened the flap and walked out, saying a mild "pardon me" to Al as he walked past, still overly polite and inoffensive but a strange light in his eyes.

Al went on in and met a scene he said he never wanted to relive. Bull was up on a bunk in what at first looked like a fetal position. Closer though, Al's eyes snapped like the strings on a cheap guitar giving out. Bull was out cold: he must have been because of the inertness of his form. But Al couldn't verify it at first because he couldn't find his head. Bull's body was twisted like a pretzel. There was no blood and no bones were broken. But every bone that amounted to anything had been curved and bent beyond bone's normal ability. Both arms were spiralled and twisted and the hands clutched the ankles from the rear. Both femurs were nearly knotted.

And the spine was anatomically impossible. It had been so sprung and articulated it took some searching to find Bull's head. But finally, Al found it in that fatal fetal mess—it had been stretched and corkscrewed and the nose thrust (it is indelicate even to write it) against the anus! Well, all Al could do at this juncture was to ascertain that Bull was alive. In fact, after trauma never before visited on mortal man, Bull appeared to be breathing normally.

Soon the place teemed with medicos of every description followed closely by taut-mouted C.I.D. investigators. Both groups were virgins: they'd never seen anything like this before. After a couple of days the specialists from Washington came somberly down, shook their heads soberly and wondered why they'd ever selected medicine as a career. They could do nothing. Not even write articles for medical journals because the army wanted it hushed up.

C.I.D. finally broke the case. Their investigators talked to Carl, but at first he wasn't forthcoming. Then they pressured, threatening him with all manner of dire consequences. Twenty years in a Texas stockade didn't appeal to Carl. So he capitulated. He told them of Bull's sadism, his passion that went before a sprawl and of Carl's frustration, and his revenge through his terrible powers. He didn't mention Lua—only that his skills had been transmitted to him by his father.

Even with the evidence in a Ft. Worth hospital they were still inclined to scoff until he brightened and asked them what the charges would be if he remedied the thing, made Bull whole again. In those days the army was capable of making an occasional astute decision. They told him that if he'd correct the situation, there would be a transfer but no charges.

Carl bought it. He went down to Ft. Worth under guard. They got the medical brass out of Bull's room and Carl went in alone. The undoing—like *tien-hsueh,* the ancient Chinese art of touching vital points—took longer than the perpetration of the original damage had. But two hours after he went in, Carl came out of the room followed by an upright but downlooking Bull.

Groucho Marx once asked, "Who do you believe, your own eyes or me?"

Well, the 20 high-rankers in the corridor believed their eyes. It was unbelievable. But they had to believe, rationality being what it is.

As for Bull, he was elongated again but a totally different person. The fire had been damped when Charon got himself dumped and nearly drowned in the good river Styx.

*Kahuna Anatomy Leaves Experts Aghast*

# IX

# MAMA SU

*As we wax hot in faction*
*In battle we wax cold;*
*Wherefore men fight not as they fought*
*In the brave days of old.*
— Macauley, *Horatius*

Major H. Loyne, who headed Britain's MI5's close combat training for 20 secret years made the famous W. E. Fairbairn look like Tess Trueheart, Dick Tracy's old moll. Loyne was only 5 foot 5 inches but 190 pounds sat on it and he was fabulous at four inches. The "H" stood for "harm" (it actually was "Harry") for he was injury incarnate. Fists, elbows, forehead, and hips, a true technician of trauma.

In the thirties he had been a spy in remote Yunnan, in the forties in Yenan, and in the fifties in Egypt. He was the only man alive who had death warrants out on him signed by Chiang Kai-shek, Mao Tse-tung, and King Farouk, disrespectively.

Loyne's skills included tuition from grand masters of shaolin in Honan and ninjutsu and judo in Tokyo. He taught me a great deal. I once watched him work over a pachyderm who had been seeking fistic satori for a fortnight; Loyne put him into nirvana in 15 seconds. An onlooking pansy gasped "Goodness." Loyne looked at him and quipped a la Mae West (when another dolly murmured "Goodness" at Mae's diamonds), "Goodness had nothing to do with it."

Loyne was sharp. He knew that some teachers will cheat a little.

"You have to be wary in what you accept. Now I'm something of an expert and I get fooled less than most. But even I have been jobbed. There is the story of a woman who made a paradigmatic chocolate cake. No one could duplicate it. On her deathbed she confessed that she'd left one ingredient out of the published recipe. Boxers will do that to you. They'll often tell you *almost* everything. You have to fill in, extrapolate. And if you've got the experience and if you're lucky you can do it."

I asked: "Is smart better than lucky?"

"Don't you believe it," he said, "I'd rather be lucky than smart any day. The smart ones are all on that plane that just went down: the lucky ones missed it and are drinking that elixir from Milwaukee and eyeing the waitress with the ball-bearing hips."

Another of Loyne's students was Shaw Desmond, the Irish poet and dramatist, who was a great believer in reincarnation and whose earliest memories, he said, were of fighting as a Roman gladiator and later as a steersman on a Viking ship. Desmond learned something, for at Albert Hall in London one night he was able to drop two men *without touching them.*

But temperamentally, he and Loyne were oceans apart and they soon parted. Later, Desmond refused to acknowledge Loyne. In *Pilgrim to Paradise* Desmond wrote:

> I had made one observation in the life about me which was to have formidable results and which, combined with a lust for the perfect body, had sent me into the "ring," and was now to send me on to the wrestling mat. This observation was that even if you had all the brain and even "guts" in the world, it availed nothing in face of a physical opponent who knew how to use his "dukes" and his feet. I still know of no situation so spiritually destructive to one's self-respect or so dreadful as for the man of brain to find himself helpless in face of superior physical force. I had experienced this in a grave-yard, of all places, and had taken my secret oath that never again should I find myself in such a position, and I heard of a secret art of death known as *ju-jutsu.*
>
> But where to find a teacher? Not having time to go to Japan, where alone it could be taught, and most urgently desiring "death in the Fingers," I developed, *pro tem,* a jujutsu of my own, which included not only death in the fingers but in the toes, elbows, or any old place with sharp corners. Strangely enough, I never thought of using a revolver or a knife, although at that English public school I had once decided to shoot the reverend head through his belly, being prevented by the hand of God or the Devil, for even now I cannot decide which.

Ungrateful clod.

Loyne was a fighter but also a gifted linguist and scholar. He remains the

*Major Loyne's Explosive Foot*

greatest living authority on Chinese dirty jokes and even compiled a volume of them only to lose the manuscript in Shanghai in 1946. He was also one of only two Caucasians fluent in the Uighur language of Sinkiang.

He knew Japanese, of course. And living amongst that race he came away with decided views on the vaunted samurai tradition.

"There is something to be said for it," he said. "Remember the story of the 47 *ronin,* samurai who had lost their lord by treachery and vowed revenge? How one, to put the enemy off guard, pretended to be a drunken sot? Well, later they avenge their master and then all commit harakiri. Afterwards, a boy, weary and dusty, travels to the tombstone of the *ronin* who had pretended to degrade himself and says aloud, 'I saw you drunk in front of a whorehouse in Kyoto and I thought you a faithless soldier and I spat in your face. I now offer atonement.' So saying, the youth slit his belly. I really don't think much of the 47 *ronin,* but this boy—he had style.

I agreed and put in my two-cents worth: "Correct. The chivalry of the samurai was impinged on by the rigors of the caste system then in vogue. He could be grand and courteous to one of his kind—or, of course, a superior— but this chivalry did not apply to those beneath him. My kick against Bushido is essentially the same as that against caste everywhere: privilege precluded kindness and compassion. He could by law slaughter a peasant on the spot for mere "disrespect." This example of chivalry in Bushido was called *kirisute yomen* ("cutting and leaving"). Such veins of inhumanity run through all cultures but especially those in which caste has been formalized. Oscar Williams, the poet, asks: 'You hear of people dying of this and that, but did you ever hear of anyone dying of compassion?'"

Loyne came back with real insight. "The samurai blade must feel only silk or the body of an opponent (sex or violence symbols, eh?). His strength was in patience, which meant holding back seven emotions: hate, adoration, joy, anxiety, anger, grief, and fear. If he could reserve these seven he believed that he would come to understand things and find harmony in life. But this wasn't life: it was a gray sort of existence. Emotions like lives, are in the living."

"Of course you know," I said, "we in the West had our own silly samurai traditions even after Cervantes in his burlesque celebrated the end of the age of chivalry. Writers at the turn of the century, intent on preaching the virtues of cold showers and continence merely shoveled guilt galore for the next two generations. One, Professor F.C. Fowler, in his *Life: How to Enjoy and How to Prolong It,* was death on self-abuse. He wrote that every time a boy expends semen, he drains his system of more vital energy than if he were to lose two ounces of the purest life blood in his body. Fowler could tell a masturbator by his facial features—he was a lonely man—and believed that the "solitary vice" was what peopled the insane asylums.

The toughest men Loyne had met, he said, were the Gurkhas, "those little brown tribesmen from Nepal who are the kindest killers in the world. They've been fighting for others for 160 years. Their battle cry is *Ayo Gurkhali* (The Gurkas are upon you). The old myth about them never unsheathing their terrible *kukri* (knife) without drawing blood is just that, a myth. They use it to peel potatoes. And did you know, John, that they all hail from one town, Gorkha?"

I responded, "Shades of shaolin and t'ai-chi, the hard and soft boxing, respectively, of China coming from two small places in Honan."

He went on, "These wiry little guys are so tough that in World War II when a Gurka unit was first asked to volunteer for paratroop service, their troubled captain asked the British advisor if the planes could drop the men from a lower height to lessen the risk of injuries. The Britisher then hastily explained that each man would have a parachute!"

I smiled. He continued: "The Gurkhas have thick skulls. John Masters, the novelist, saw a sergeant bend down to tie his bootlace just behind a particularly fractious mule. The mule let drive, and both iron-shod hoofs smashed with murderous force into the sergeant's temple. He complained of a headache all afternoon. The mule went dead lame."

This talk occurred in a Hamburg nightspot. I was taping it. We got on to how we were aging and he quoted Ezra Pound: "I was quite strong — at least they said so — / The young men at the sword-play; / But I have put aside this folly, being gay / In another fashion that more suiteth me."

Just then a young buck bulking over 200 pounds walked up, picked up my tape recorder and made for the exit. He didn't make it. Loyne intercepted him and knocked him unconscious with a blow that I didn't see.

He sauntered back smiling and sixty.

"Hell, Loyne, you haven't lost it. How do you do it?" I asked.

To which he gave me the classic line from Pound's "San Vio": "Old powers rise and do return to me."

Loyne had some fabulous adventures, but none so eerie and frightening as the one involving a female Kahuna priestess with the unlikely tag of "Mama Su." But it's his story, let him tell it. Paraphrasing Papa, draw your chair up close to the edge of the precipice and Harry will tell you a story.

*        *        *

Having arrived at one of the Tahitian Kingdom's more obscure (and therefore still beautiful) outer islands, I was in no mood for the temptations of the martial art. Other seductions were abundant in the living sea, spectacular plant life, and an attractive group of warm, open human beings. A career of teaching Asian fighting arts had given me cause to ponder the nature and substance of the many twisted human forms I had encountered. One had but to teach for a few years to have seen and comprehended the paranoid violet gaze of the all-too-typical student who bears the burden of his endless search for a "masculinity" yet unproven to himself, or the "teachers" who bore the invisible wounds of a private reality called psychosis. Nor could I ignore the youthful taste for blood which I had seen in myself and some other martial artists.

All of this threw a cruel betrayal in the face of the high romantic ideals of Budo we had clung to from boyhood. To be sure not all was so grim. Many fine, indeed noble personalities still inhabit the *dojo,* and the universities now flow forth with acute young minds trained in educational martial art ready to serve society rather than decimate others. Nevertheless, the discipline and its adherents are, let's say, somewhat heavy, and the old fighter healing ancient wounds in the warm smile of a friendly sun is, in no way, eager for tales of combat lore.

Thus as I reclined on a solitary beach, and admired myself for a decorous tan bought cheaply in a few hours of joyous surfing, I had nothing more serious to contemplate than whether indeed I should once again ride my noble stick (surfboard) on the altogether perfect curls which were even now being produced in infinite sets by a generous ocean, or, whether I should lust after the numerous fish which boiled up inside a near reef. The Polynesian sling is a superb instrument, and like all true weapons, is brilliant in its simplicity. The weapon is composed of a narrow barbed fish spear to which at the blunt end are attached two loops of rubber tubing. The loops are wrapped around thumb and forefinger, then stretched so that the entwined hand can grasp the spear in midshaft creating a hunting projectile of taut, spontaneous energy. When aimed at a fish the shaft is simply released, and said fish is instantly liberated of all earthly *karma.*

Thinking myself alone and feeling the weight of the spear, I began the movements of a *kata* (form) of the priestly *Hozuin Ryu So-jutsu* (spear art), a fluid and expressive art I had learned at the feet of Draeger *Sensei*, perhaps the only westerner alive who could be truly called a samurai.

Entranced as I was in the harmonious flow of circular and linear which is intrinsic to this art, I was rather surprised and a bit embarrassed to turn in midpivot and find company. There standing at leeward was the grizzled Scots skipper of the excellent gaff-rigged schooner which had lately deposited me ashore in this paradise, and was now taking aboard a cargo of copra. At his elbow stood an athletic Island kid who was quite obviously bursting with fascination.

The captain was himself a fighter of some repute in the south seas. He had wrestled in the catch trade when there were shooters rather than bluffers in the ring. Rumor in Samoa had it that the year before, the good captain had disposed of a karate *sandan* who had crossed the skipper by his rude words and unsavory attentions toward a Fijian lady. The unfortunate restaurant where this occurred received grievous structural damage when the old seaman, then on the hard side of fifty, in his cups and having been somewhat angered by two kicks to the head, sent the karateman bursting through the kitchen wall. When questioned at some length by mutual friends, the old skipper waxed poetic and answered somewhat arcanely with the right allusion to Brother Dylan, "Just then the kitchen exploded in boiling fat, / Food was flying everywhere / —I left without my hat."

Now any enlightened mind would see in the wrinkled map of the face on this old seasnake that he was truly a living cultural treasure, and therefore pay due heed to his requests. So it was that I repented of my fast from training and finally gave in when Captain Ben Reed asked me in a personal way on the strength of favors longstanding, if I would "Teach this young pup some tricks. He's blood-kin to me, and an eager lad."

Yes, I would, and so we practiced *sojutsu* for a long afternoon. The next morning brought my new disciple with gifts of broiled fish and *poi* which invoked once again in me the response to teach. The martial traditions holds that a sincere student may learn in return for service — no money need pass through our hands. That bond holds me still it seems, in obligation to the memory of my first master who taught me his art in return for my clumsy and rather comical attempts to sweep the *dojo*.

Although I was poor, *Sensei* tendered me his vast art of judo and jujutsu in return for my sincerity. Yet what he really taught me, I realized years later was the kind of precious qualities which can exist in a human relationship based upon learning. Real teachers can't resist true students and this youth, whose name was Pelakai, had skills of his own in the art of Siva — the Samoan knife dance. So well trained was he in his art of martial choreography that by the second day he was able to perform a basic set of southern shaolin boxing.

I was a bit amazed at his progress, and asked him the source of his superb training. He responded quite simply that his mother had taught him! His mother, it developed, was matriarch of the entire island, having descended from a royal lineage which had once contended for the throne. Its illustrious heritage could boast of having given seed to the nobility of Kauai in Hawaii. I, of course, asked after the whereabouts of this great lady, and was informed that she was presently attending to a difficult childbirth on the far side of the island.

She was, it turned out, chief matron of midwifery, an ancient yet sophisticated medical art involving massage, breath control, and applied psychotherapy. In addition, she was high Kahuna of the traditional psychic religion in those islands, and a mistress of the secret martial art which was a direct manifestation of that faith. I was, of course, astounded at my good fortune, for here possibly was the actual origin of Hawaiian Lua, a nearly extinct martial art taught only to a few pure Polynesians.

I was alive with anticipation and questioned Pelakai so closely that he grew fearful at having in his enthusiasm broken the family code of secrecy. He begged that I not disclose his indiscretion and refused to discuss the subject further. All was not lost, however, and upon questioning the skipper that night I learned that he was married to the great lady's younger sister and was pleased on my behalf to wangle an invitation to a feast four days hence. The matriarch was known to those who loved her (which meant nearly everyone) as Mama Su, an affectionate abbreviation of her long and nearly unpronounceable given name.

The skipper, who had known her for years, disclosed that Mama Su was quite well traveled and indeed had been something of a rake in her wild youth. She had journeyed throughout Indonesia and the South Pacific and mastered a variety of traditional disciplines, including the fighting arts. Stories abound concerning her exploits, the most famous of which occurred in Suva during 1943 when she encountered a brutal rape being committed by four French marines. The conflict was short and vicious, the results were not pretty to behold. One attacker escaped to tell the tale. Of the three armed with knives who chose to stand and fight, one was killed on the spot, one suffered a three-month total neurological paralysis, and the other was blinded for life. The younger one, who wisely fled, swore that she had flattened one of his comrades from a distance of eight feet! This, of course, was greeted with disbelief. Yet the tale intrigued me, and I became determined to witness her art.

When at last the feast occurred I met this noble lady amid a celebration of life surrounded by her numerous children and kin-folk. It was an atmosphere permeated by an aura of warmth and love. She stood at least six feet and weighed upwards of 280 pounds. To my analytic eye the contours of her magnificent body were rotund yet smooth and well packed like a Sumo wrestler's physique. She was a great and vital human being and radiated me, a stranger, with her rainbow smile.

After a memorable night of new friendships bound in feast, dance, and

*Mama Su in Her Arcadia*

song we sat down by the fire — Pelakai, the skipper, Mama and I, and the time came for me to ask to see her art. With a brief withering glare of reproof at her betraying and now disconsolate son, she turned to me once again smiling, and politely refused.

"Our people," said she, "have lived in peace for generations and wisely put away the crafts of war; we envy none and give no race cause to resent our small share of this earth. That our fighting art should survive in secret, taught to but a few in each generation, is an act of deference to our revered ancestors who willed it so. You are our guest and I would never insult you. It is necessary to understand, however, that ours is an art of the spirit which calls up demons from the belly of humankind. Once *the angries* are aroused they demand blood, and are never easily put to rest."

Then, looking straight into the depth of my soul, she said: "You must, I am sure, know this from within yourself — I will say no more of fighting."

That night as the children and kinfolk went one by one off to bed she sat with me by the glowing coals and gave me her wisdom through secret knowledge about myself that I had never dared share. The Mama was an avid chewer of betel nut and as she sat in deep reflection she would occasionally pause and bestow a sizzling chaw into the glowing coals and then proceed to expose for me, with profound insight and compassion, the raw nerve of my innermost feelings.

We put to sea a day later bound for Suva, and on that day as we said goodbye, I felt that precious martial arts knowledge had slipped through my fingers, yet in a far more personal sense I had gained a degree of wisdom.

This might have been the end of our tale and an unfortunate termination of some important anthropological investigation had not an unfortunate event in the Mama's family dramatically intervened. Of her six sons, three had left the island with their mother's blessing to seek a larger life. One son is a student of agriculture in New Zealand and one is presently completing a doctoral dissertation in oceanography at UCLA. The other, aged 18, became a long-haired searcher after truth.

Twelve days after the feast we came ashore during a full moon with bad tidings of this third son. He had, it seems, been beaten, publicly ridiculed, and finally jailed by the police in Papeete; a very rare event in that warm city. When we arrived at the family compound, the atmosphere was dark indeed, everyone had left in the face of Mama's sorrowful wrath.

That night, attended by four Kahuna, Mama made serious magic: herb compounds were consumed, chickens slaughtered, and incredible amounts of psychic energy released. Although apprehensive, Ben and I stayed, caught between dread and fascination. At the climax of these rites the entire firelit

compound was enveloped by psychic vibrations of incredible intensity. All I
could do was sit there and murmur repeatedly, "Cor."

Mama Su rose and the other Kahuna quickly moved out of the circle of
light created by the fire. She began to move slowly at first in rhythmic circular
configurations which I recognized at once as a sophisticated martial form. I
was transfixed as the form developed. The classic elements were all there: the
stance changes, the energy flow, and the subtle yin/yang dualities which
indelibly mark the higher art. As she began to move faster, open hand
operations emerged in dazzling defensive patterns — no fists nor kicks and
few blows save for double palms (which seemed quite close to Chinese
butterfly palms: *po pai cheng*). This simple description fails to convey the
tremendous expression of psychophysiological power she unleashed that
night; after a series of baffling pivots and turns she would focus and blow
forth an explosion of breath. It was as if the *ch'i* in pure form were erupting
directly out of her body rather than through the medium of focused punch
or kick.

Ben shook me out of my daze, saying, "This is no place for us, Harry!"
Remembering his presence I turned and saw a look of utter dread. In the far
corner of the yard a tethered pig began to squeal from its own sense of terror.
Mama stopped as if distracted and stared at us through red swollen eyes, and
said simply; "I have *the angries* . . . go." The veins on her face and neck were
pulsating and she loomed before us like a mythic embodiment of her people's
bloody past. Although visibly shaken myself I said, "I must see this." Ben
gripped my arm and cursed. "I've seen this before. For God's sake, *come!*" I
broke his grip and Ben whispered finally: "Then stay, you fool, if pry you
must, but *listen:* if anything happens, lie down and curl up like a baby, she'll
harm no living thing which takes that shape!"

In spite of the drama that engulfed us at that instant I smiled a bit. With
my training I knew that I could if need be overcome this 44-year old woman
without injuring her seriously. I belonged to the Zup school of self-defense: I
would fight anyone any style, it was "Zup" to them. I saw Ben vanish into the
jungle, and turning once more I saw that the Mama had closed to a distance
of perhaps nine feet, the look on her face contorted and insane. Reflexively I
brought my hands into the classic *Ch'uan-fa* position. The force of the impact
literally blew me backwards off of my feet—*she had spit directly into my face!*
I had felt such force few times before—once pushing hands with a t'ai-chi
master; once during a bomb explosion in Singapore. Though stunned, years
of ingrained techniques caused me to roll backwards into a judo fall and
recover my stance. As I shifted and moved sideways into a *lost track* avoidance
of rare Mi Tsung-i, I tasted betel nut. We were both moving very fast now, I

trying desperately to turn her corner and close the distance. I managed two quick changes when a load of spittle exploded viciously on my ear and cut me off my feet. That was it—the equilibrium was gone and my nervous system reeled; I looked up into her wrathful face and instinctively curled into an abject fetal position.

The next blow never came. She paused for a moment and then wheeled away into her form, although now she moved like a large sleek animal in that exquisite instant before the kill. My ear was pounding and I had vision in only one eye. I watched her now not from fascination but in pure stark fear. The power of her rage was incredible, she moved and leaped, thrashed and turned once again—she spit wildly and I saw a large palm leaf fall as if cut by a machete. As she moved near the pig, the terrified creature jumped with fright. In almost the same instant she turned and spewed a betel nut, and it dropped as if hit by a bullet. The wretched beast lay on its side, legs quivering. She leapt forward like a lioness, picked it up by a haunch and an ear, and then to my horror *sank her teeth into its throat.* I felt rising nausea and thought I surely must be delirious: I had stupidly raised up psychological demons of combat and now a blood price was being paid—that pig, I knew, was a surrogate for *me.*

Much later her great arms gently encircled me and lifted me up to her bosom, as she carried me inside. I looked up and saw tears mixed with blood. She tenderly placed me on a mattress and covered me with a canvas, caressed me and then silently departed into the night.

The next day I awoke with a broken eardrum and a spectacular black eye. The family surrounded me with loving care and worried attention. Their friend and guest had been injured and they were profoundly sorry. This warm civilization is surely founded on sharing, love and open spirit. During the next few days I had cause to reflect with some considerable embarrassment upon my own behavior as the meddling outsider invading a holy and very personal scene of grief; and even moreover which comprised a private rite of another people's religion. How humiliating to compare myself to the numerous other white intruders: imperialists, missionaries, self-seeking adventurers all smugly claiming to bear a gift of "civilization," and all of whom when meeting a natural and wholly justifiable anger, were so quick to cast the ignorant label "primitive" upon a truly noble and refined people.

That great lady remained in her home for two days, emerging finally with her usual good humor. News had arrived from Papeete with official and profuse apologies concerning her son. High government sources close to the royal family informed her that her beloved son had been released, that the loutish police involved were being punished, and that it would not be necessary for the Mama Su to come to Papeete and retrieve her baby.

During the following month Mama Su did divulge considerable information to me concerning her art to the extent in fact that I was able to produce a credible 12-foot delivery—with diminished power, however. Considering the nature and lethal capacity of the technique, details will not be published. Copies of the technical analysis however have been placed in the Gilbey files and restricted library collections at two universities. In deference to the lady and people of her island the location will be considered privileged information. I will say however categorically that the system is internal and has some analogous relationship to Japanese *kiaijutsu* and the Chinese *ch'i-kung* of internal boxing; there are in fact some interesting training methods which have a close resemblance to an older substyle of Indonesian Pentjak-Silat.*

Historically, the system developed collaterally with classical Polynesian medicine and Tahitian hula. This art, like several other esoteric martial disciplines, has been historically kept secret to such an extent that the very name of the system is known to only a few within the higher circles of traditional Polynesian religion. The method is viewed as an exclusive cultural resource which must remain undiluted, pure, and beyond the danger of exploitation. My field interview with Mama Su was granted with the express assurance that the material was derived solely for the purpose of scientific knowledge acquisition.

At the close of my three-month sojourn on that happy island, I created bonds of affection with a sensitive people whose culture I truly admire. As I stood on the dock exchanging farewells and expressions of deep feeling I asked the Mama one final question: "What," I inquired, "is the real source of your power?" "Oh, Harry, *you* should know," she responded with a wink and a hefty slap on the nether side of her fullsome girth, *"It's all in the waist."*

---

*These are techniques that involve concentric muscular contractions within a lumbar-abdominal focus. This focus emanates from adrenocortical response triggers associated with psycho-physiologically induced secretions of epinephrine.

# X

# POP SONGS AND PA-KUA

*"Children born of fairy stock*
*Never need for shirt or frock,*
*Never want for food or fire,*
*Always get their heart's desire."*
—R. Graves

This story starts in Chicago when the going was good. Before Daley. There was a piano player there at the Blackhawk who used to bet me drinks on the vital statistics of old songs and old fighters. Jangles Ryan. He had a right hand as good as Art Tatum's but there it ended. He was forever slotted for an obscure existence of a too-toothy grin for the folks and that splendid right hand.

After keeping Jangles liquid for a couple of years, I got so I could hold my own on the old songs, particularly those of the thirties. By then he had trouble playing anything I couldn't identify and peg to a year.

He had boxed. He had a left as good as Ray Robinson's but there it ended, too. He was full of boxing stories, but music is where he shone. He introduced me to Fats Waller's greatest number, "Hog Maw Stomp", a stomp that'll stump even most Waller experts. I tried it out on the best down in New Orleans as late as 1974 and nary a one had ever heard of it.

Jangles couldn't read music. On that and other aspects of pianoing he was well back of Fatha Hines. He would brood on this sometimes. Then I'd tell him that Bix Beiderbecke who "could make a cornet sound like a girl saying yes" (Eddie Condon's felicitous phrase) couldn't read music, fingered backward, and drank himself to death, but was the best cornet player of all time. And that George Brunis, the "Wild Man of the Trombone" who died in 1974 couldn't read either. Something of a showman, he would sometimes let men stand on his chest while he played (Paul Whiteman had a trombonist, Willie Hall, who could play "Nola" while standing on his head). Brunis had a good ear and played a style of trombone no one plays anymore (as his friend, pianist Art Hodes, put it, "They play like they've been going to school"). Jangles liked hearing such things and reciprocated by giving me the inside dope on popular music.

But more important—for me and this book—he put me onto Jim Sain, saying, "John boy, you're ready for graduate work. Years ago a young fellow used to come here. Name of Jim Sain. Jim knew all the best in pop of the twenties and thirties. He was a marvel. I didn't see him for several years and it turned out he had gone to Washington where he went high in government in just a few years. Next thing I knew he came through on his way back to his dad's farm in Nebraska. Said he'd given up on Washington: it was as false as the politicians that ran it."

"We have a lot in common," I told Jangles. "It was Mencken who said that there were more clowns there than in burlesque."

Well, to make a long story shorter, Jangles gave me Jim's address and I wrote to him. Promptly (courtesy is always a good sign) he answered, telling me to come on out to Nebraska.

A week later I arrived at Jim's town, whose name he asked me to leave anonymous. Let's call it Circleville. A fair sized place, it wasn't prepossessing. It once had had a choice between having a university branch or a penitentiary. The city fathers had opted for the latter.

Now New York, that nickel town (another way of describing it is to call it a "three-day town"), claims to be our cultural center the same way it claims to have the toughest citizenry. But the midwest is more cultured, smarter, and tougher. The smart part needs no elucidation what with Papa, Cully Sandburg, and the rest. The tough part was proved out in Circleville. The place reeked of violence. You could taste it in the air.

Jim met me at the small rail station. His greeting was authentic, no restraint in his smile. I could see Jim Sain was more than a farmer. His hands were ungnarled and he had a soft handshake. I asked myself: how does he farm 165 acres, harvest 6,000 bushels of corn and manage 40 head of stock with these lily hands? I found out later. His face was unweathered and all smiles. When I commented on it, he quoted Bernard Shaw to the effect that a smiling man seldom shoots.

He was bright as the sun after a matinee Western on Saturday afternoons. He moved lithely and was agile as a wolverine—not at all like a sod buster. His walk should have given him away. His head was erect, the shoulders immobile, and he walked from the hips down. Easy but firm steps. Nothing military about it. In this macho era Americans think John Wayne's amble is the acme of masculinity, but it's really the exaggerated sprung walk of a homosexual. If you want to see a warrior's walk, watch the Japanese actor Mifune in any of his sword classics. Or, if you could have been so lucky, you could have watched Jim Sain.

From his first words you knew you were speaking to that rarity—a whole man. Intensely humble, extensively wise. It is said that an intelligent man knows others, a wise man knows himself. Put him down then as both intelligent and wise.

To give you an idea of his acumen, he did crosswords with a fountain pen while delineating for me Heisenberg's theory of indeterminacy!

He showed me around the small farm. I tried not to reflect my boredom. But I wasn't content till we got back inside and onto a subject other than agricultural.

Finally we were out of the alfalfa and inside and there was a roaring fire going in the huge old fireplace and we were ensconced in old morris chairs and had hold of comfortable cognacs. Loaded for bear, we got down to the business of reviewing the twenties and thirties song-wise.

But first Jim threw me glaringly off balance by saying he had heard of my combat skills. "Why do you fight, John?," he asked politely—but it was cotton over steel. He wanted to know the answer to a question every person in the martial arts must answer properly and honestly to the only real questioner —himself. But I had it made. It was a cakewalk.

"I don't anymore," I started, "it's a bootless enterprise. Even in the old days when I thought I had to be competitive, and the old zest of adventure and triumph boiled in my veins, even then I was careful that no innocent suffered and no guilty bird suffered too much. In those days it was like learning a trade or taking a Ph.D. in the martial, so it had another dimension, too, quite beyond the immediate and the sanguine."

"And you have no more to learn?" he questioned.

"Hell, as far as that's concerned, there's no end to it. No, the longer I studied and the more fluent I became, the more I realized that young guy I used to know in Mobile was right. He used to pump gas down there and was a pretty fair boxer. In an area where they're notoriously light hitters, he had a right hand that would stop a streetcar. But he couldn't jab and that ended him. Always bet the boxer, not the slugger."

"What was it he said that so impressed you?" he queried softly, bringing me back to square one.

"Right. Well sir, he quoted me Plato, who said something to the effect that a fight undertaken *for any reason* is an admission of failure. Man, he would say, is a thinking reed. If you go the physical route, it means that you lack either the rational or emotional equipment to do it in style, that is, non-physically."

Then Jim Sain asked me if violence could ever be condoned. What about killing if done in self-defense and done "sacramentally?"

"The act of violence is itself a rationalization. It should be avoided. There is really no excuse for fighting beyond one's immediate family or a stranger unfairly set upon. Pride certainly is no excuse. I've 'cowarded' out of more fights than I fought—and in my time I fought a lot—simply because the guy was fouled up and needed something other than a beating. So I fooled him by letting him believe he scared me."

Enough of me. I turned the discussion back to him. Between what he said and what I heard from other sources later, I learned that he had been brilliant in school but had turned down a Phi Beta Kappa key: he rejected it, saying it was a barbaric thing attached to a pompous rite. On graduation day when they called his name up yonder as one of five graduating with highest honors, he wasn't there.

"Whoever would dress up in caps and gowns and listen to tired irrelevancies didn't have education. They lacked it," he said. "Besides," and his eyes twinkled, "at that time I was under the grandest apple tree with the fairest damsel who was telling me the most remarkable things about Amy Lowell, the poet."

Then we talked about bureaucrats, a species I had always regarded as beneath mention. But he had deep feelings on the breed and dwelt on them at some length.

He had worked as a government bureaucrat for a time, but the institutional insidiousness of bureaucratism caused him to jump clear at the first opportunity. He thought bureaucracy man's greatest enemy.

"On the national level there is almost no decision in recent years I agree with. Civil liberties, the economy, the war machine, Vietnam—you name it, decisions on all of 'em were wrong. They had to be, given the bureaucratic ooze out of which they emerged. You can't blame the political parties: the bankrupt Republicans with their privilege, power, and fear, and the inept Democrats who confuse Henry Jackson with a liberal. They are bad enough but no worse than they should be. But the blame really has to go to that devitalizing devil—bureaucracy.

"One scholar defines bureaucracy as the most efficient means of reducing feedback and producing entropy. But bureaucracy is not chaos: it is too epicene. Chaos, after all, ain't all bad. All good poets have to have some in them. No, a bureaucracy is too nothing even to be nihilistic. It makes the Taoist *wu-wei* (inaction) look like a Chinese fire drill."

He poured a generous libation of cognac, relit his cigar with a kitchen match, and smiled.

From these promising beginnings we moved into music and joyed away three days. Jim's first comments on the subject I still remember.

"I knew a professor once with a variety of interests: he was a first-rate musician, chess-player, and even dabbled in self-defense. But he didn't like jazz, called it an 'explosion of puberty.' It had, he said, some interesting tone-color facets but lousy harmony, form, counterpoint, and no original melody—it cribbed from the masters. I told him to listen to Don Redman's 'Chant of the Weed.' He said he would. And must have because I haven't heard from him since. Sore loser."

That set the stage for a beautiful time. Jangles had been right: Jim was a genius and I was a novice. He had a piano and could play well enough, and he had a superb record collection. So we ate, slept, walked, and talked music and it was funsville for the both of us.

The last night was a bit different but even more fun. We ran into a feisty little bird in town who turned out to be Jim's Uncle Herman. The old soul was drizzly drunk, which I came to learn was his usual condition. Now and then, Jim said, he drank beer in an unsuccessful attempt to stay sober. He liked the juice and it seemed to like him—it deterred him nowise from doing the chores on his 24-acre farm. Add to which, Jim said, Uncle Herman was a cantankerous bastard when sober. I must own to an adversion to dips but I'm the first to admit that my bias may be all wrong. Look at it medically: you see more old drunks than you do old doctors. That has to give you pause.

(At one point during my stay the old geezer smiled up at me with his rheumy eyes that betrayed a liver gone with alcohol and croaked, "If I'd a knowed I was going to live this long, I'd a taken better care of myself!")

But right now Uncle Herman was crying softly, all the while wiping his eyes on the cuff of a shirt that probably was blue once. When Jim asked the reason, the ancient one grunted that the boys down at Welch's had been at him again. Apparently he was the butt of all the jokes the yokels could think up at the main local watering place.

"But did you tell them that I said to knock it off?" Jim asked.

"I did," Uncle Herman said, "and they told me to tell you to go to hell."

Jim sighed and told the old boy to push off home and that he'd see what could be done. Herman agreed and shambled off, but with some parting advice through bleary lips: "O.K., boy, but watch those Fancher boys. They're meaner 'n hell."

Welch's was one of four taverns in the town, each a shot away from the others. And one church. A felicitous ratio as it turned out—there were four times as many reasons to get drunk as to get religion there. For despite the ever-latent violence, the town was so dead that dying was redundant. The one church wasn't much; it was almost as tough as Welch's, at high mass you could smoke in the last five rows. It pretty well epitomized the old saying that anything good a preacher'll find first. Welch's disdained the church and the other taverns. You couldn't even buy a coke in Welch's. It was a tough place in a tough town. Hell, we almost got hit just crossing the street in front of the place by a car with a bumper sticker that read: "Honk if you want a punch in the nose."

Well, we went into Welch's about 9 and the joint was already jumping. Jim was in his work clothes and I wasn't much fancier. We lucked out on a small table against the wall and ordered beer from a blousy blond, a disheveled veteran of the quick grab and go. We sat and talked, sizing the place up but pretending real interest only in ourselves. The din was so great that the jukebox cacophony came through to us only in those moments when a majority of those present all inhaled at once.

The crowd was free-wheeling but after a time we noticed that the hilarity centered on a table at a once remove from us where five men—four burly and one slender—were boozing it up. Those birds didn't own the place but they might as well have. They were an oligarchy, exacting tribute, bestowing favors, and instilling fear and obedience in everyone. Even the sheriff, a wisp of a guy packing a rod he'd have to hold in both hands, came in right after we got there and kow-towed nervously to their table before drinking a beer at the bar—he wasn't invited to join them—and hitching himself back up to go out and look for sin. He probably came in once a night as a general rule to see if there was anyone they wanted shot.

I nodded toward the table and delineated its contents for Jim. "I will bet," I began, "that at yon table sit Herman's tormentors. Notice how no one bumps their chairs while we're getting seasick from being joggled every ten seconds."

He said nothing. I had been raised in an environment where you didn't wait for assent to keep talking. Silence gave assent—and sometimes the only opportunity. I started to speak but just then the blonde came back with our second round.

"Those folks look like they're having fun," I commented to the blonde. She put the beer down and nodded.

"Them's the Fanchers: Junior, Walt, Fred, Luke and Phil. They're here most nights. Always sit in the same chairs. Walt's the one in the red shirt. Don't mean no harm but they can get playful." She laughed obscenely as she turned away: hell yes, she knew how playful they could be.

We drank and got back to music.

Jim said, "The important thing was not whether a song or arrangement was jazz or pop but whether it was swing."

"I hear you."

"Swing is the spirit making circles and it can be communicated. It makes your toes tap, your hands clap, and your soul sing. Fats Waller was once asked 'What is swing?' by an American matron and Fats answered: 'Lady, if you got to ask, you ain't got it.'"

"Yeah," I came in, "Louis Armstrong and jazz erroneously figure in that story nowadays."

He continued: "A lot of jazz—for example, the progressive garbage of Dizzy Gillespie and others—did not swing, and a lot of pop did."

We ordered another round and the blonde brought them, put them down, wagged her hennaed head at the Fancher table, and said: "Walt Fancher wants to talk to one of you."

Jim didn't hear her, I guess. He continued his dissertation. "The bureaucrats got into the game trying to define jazz and if you didn't make the cut you were pop, which was by definition, of course, bad. But swing is of the spirit and can't be contained. A good musician can produce swing with sand blocks, spoons, or even a comb."

"You're right. Remember Red McKenzie and his comb? I'll never forget his rendition of 'Arkansas Blues.'"

"Or a voice could do the job of instruments in producing swing." He took a drink and went on. "Al Bowlly fooling around with da dee da dee da on 'You Ought To Be in Pictures,' or Bing Crosby or Connie Boswell."

The waitress had sniffed and gone over to the Fanchers. I nodded toward their table. "She's tattling on us, you know." Then I returned to context by asking his view of the Boswell Sisters.

"Only the best. They broke up after 1935, otherwise they would've made it much bigger commercially than they did. Which is something because they were too good to be commercial."

He looked at his hands.

"Out of New Orleans, they were white but when they sang it seemed to come out of ebony soul. Connie is the best known, but all three were pros in the fullest sense. And they were a team." He paused and I came on like Superman.

"I agree. For all the fireworks in their vocals, they never rehearsed. They exploded into a song and as one British critic once wrote 'They take a tune between their teeth and shake it like a terrier with a piece of old rag.'"

He smiled. He liked that. But I knew he wouldn't let it lay.

He didn't: "I remember that quote," he said. "The same critic commented on Jimmy Dorsey's clarinet on their version of 'When I Take My Sugar To Tea' that it was 'a girl running down the steps of a jazz club in a tight skirt.' But the point I was making is that swing may ebb a bit from time to time but it will last. And when anthropologists in future analyze the broken shards and other artifacts of what passes for culture with us, they will hold swing up as our finest ornament."

I interrupted. "Even the banal, commercial stuff?"

He frowned. "Style is everything. Garbage handled with style can be a symphony. Some very good singers had to sing some very ephemeral material and rather than it disparaging them, they enhanced it."

"Give me a for instance," I asked.

"Sure, take Mildred Bailey. One of the finest who ever lived. She was pure stylesville. Once asked whether what she was singing was jazz or pop, she answered: 'Hell honey, I just sing.' And she did. For contrast listen to the tear-drenched 'Heaven Help This Heart of Mine,' a ballad, and 'Bob White,' one of the most rollicking swing numbers ever. She had a real range and she never short-changed on any number."

"You're making quite a defense for pop. Wasn't a lot of it maudlin and schmaltzy?"

"Granted, but gosh, it had life. Much of it was corn but we forget that people live that way. George Jean Nathan, the best drama critic we ever had, once spoke of a woman who was the kind who knew the words of old songs, as a gal he could dig. Now Guy Lombago and Lawrence Smelk can send you to tiredsville pretty quick, but there is a large body of old pop that still gets played. Critics put it down as sentimental. Maybe. But a lot of sentiment has the virtue of honesty. It may be gauche and overdone but it usually is more honest than the 'with-it' critics who live mean little squalid Playboy magazine lives of emptiness and despair."

The youngest member of the group kept looking over at us, talking all the while to the others. Finally, he came over to check us out. He was a mix of brazen and bashful as he dumped himself into one of the chairs at our table.

I was saying to Jim: "Did you ever hear Annette Hanshaw?"

(Junior Fancher fidgeted).

"Yup, real sprightly. I particularly liked 'You're the One I Care For.'"

"Migosh," I said, "I haven't heard that one for more than 30 years but I bet I could still sing three-fourths of the lyrics."

Jim's eyes danced. He was hoping I would, and he wanted to see how the kid would handle the lyrics on top of the waiting.

But I didn't. Instead I asked: "What other white vocalists did you like?"

"Where you fellas from?" Junior broke in with as friendly a voice as a person packed with pugnacity could muster.

Normally I'll "friendly" this type out of their jocks but I prize courtesy and he had interrupted us. So this time I wasn't in the mood. Jim wasn't either. Looking through Fancher, he answered: "Helen Ward with BG in the mid-30's who had the warmest vibrato and some of the best phrasing I can remember. The two Lees, Morse and Wiley, were also great."

"Yeah," I took the ball and ran with it, "compare the job each does on 'It's the Girl.' And for pure merriment Lee Morse did two other classics, 'I've Got Five Dollars' and 'Old Man Sunshine, Little Boy Bluebird.' "

"I know 'em both," Jim came in.

By this time Junior had gotten glassy-eyed and was fit to eat the table. He was hearing strange sissy stuff and he was being disregarded. He didn't like either. Knowing he was the cynosure of all eyes in the place, he blurted out: "Ain't seen you here before."

It was nice-guy time. I positively beamed on him and said in my best Nebraskan patois: "We ain't been here afore."

Then back to Jim who completely disregarded the boy. "Here's a tough one. Name Helen Morgan's best number."

He shook his head as though I had done something sleazy. "You didn't think I would say 'Bill' or 'My Man' did you?"

I said nothing and he went on. "Well they were good, but not the best. My favorite is 'Sand in My Shoes!' "

This shocked hell out of me. It was uncanny. With our similarity of taste, we could have been Siamese twins.

I asked: "And your Lee Wiley favorite was probably the one she liked best, 'Down to Steamboat Tennessee'?"

His eyes lit up and he nodded, "True, but 'Any Time, Any Day, Anywhere' was a close second."

Junior Fancher grunted and got up, trying to look tougher than he was, and forced a tight smile: "Well now have fun, but watch the broads—some of these old boys don't like strangers horning in on their gals."

I joked that neither of us was horny and he laughed, not meaning it, looked at me like a dog looks at a fire hydrant, and went back to his table.

I turned back to Jim as truculence trod off. "Remember 1936?"

"Like my social security number," he laughed.

"OK. Can you name ten songs that were in the top 20 played most frequently on radio that year?"

He sipped his beer and turned mentally inward.

"Easy. 'When Did You Leave Heaven', 'When I'm With You', 'Did I Remember', 'Until the Real Thing Comes Along', 'The Way You Look

Tonight', 'All My Life', 'Stomping at the Savoy', 'Alone', 'You', 'Would You?' and my favorite, 'Robins and Roses'."

"That's eleven," I said ruefully, "I'm glad I didn't ask you for all 20!"

I looked up and there was the top of the clan, Walt himself. He stood there, huge, self-important, aggressive, spoiling for battle. He stood there . . . and stood there. Neither of us paid him any mind. And after standing there on his size 14 gunboats for two or three minutes he began to feel uncertain. Mainly because of what he was hearing.

Jim says: "What was the best band you ever heard?"

I respond: "Sweet or swing?"

He says: "Let's start with swing."

"Then that's easy," I said. "Ray Noble's 1933 Mayfair bunch."

He: "Not Claude Thornhill's 1941 group?"

Me: "Nope, that was a one-song bunch, worth seeing but not worth going to see."

"Yeah, Sam Johnson," he drawled, "'Snowflake' was an interesting number."

(The mountain shifted and nervously hitched up his trousers. This was the damnedest thing he'd ever heard.)

Jim continued: "I agree with you; Noble was a consummate artist as an arranger. He had good personnel—and best of all he had Al Bowlly."

"If you had to pick the best four Noble numbers, what would they be?" I asked.

He mused, "That wouldn't be easy: there were so many good ones. But I guess I'd put 'By the Fireside', 'Love is the Sweetest Thing,' 'Hold My Hand,' and 'You're Driving Me Crazy' right up there."

"Darned good choices," I said.

By this time big fella had had it. He coughed and boomed out: "You 'uns havin' fun?"

Jim gave him a look like he was a side dish he hadn't ordered, and went on: "How good really was Al Bowlly?"

"Only the best," I replied.

He: "Better than Crosby, Eddy Howard, early Sinatra?"

Me: "Easily better than syrupy Eddy and more real than Sinatra, although he didn't have the gimmicks."

"One of you guys Jim Sain?" roared big 'un, and now the whole place got quiet.

Jim looks at him sweetly, says: "That's me, but I'm talking to a friend."

At this, Biggie said, "You're talking to me," but he was thinking too much of the words and the effort impeded the action of his massive right mitt which swung up to take Jim by the collar front and yank him to attention. The hand got up to the collar and thought it closed on it, but ended up holding a fistful of air. Jim had moved his head back three inches. So Fancher stood there with his gargantuan fist clenched tight on nothing.

It was ludicrous . . . and dangerous. I knew Fancher was committed now—he had to act. I relaxed my shoulders. But I also had a funny feeling: how had Jim escaped that clutch-and-rise, all the time so unconcerned about it?

For he was oblivious of Fancher and was still talking. "Now as to Bing, that's tough. He was like a hedgehog—he had only one trick but it was a good one."

I figured if he could nonchalant it, so could I. "Bowlly could do more?"

Jim said, "Mebbe. But I wouldn't say it was better than Bing. Can't we have two champs?"

He barely got the words out when Walt picked up our table and heaved it against the wall. That was where I was, but that was O.K.—I'm good against tables. I took it on my forearms. What was bad was that it blocked my vision of what Walt next did to Jim.

Or tried to do.

By the time I got the table off me and moved forward to "rescue" Jim it was too late. The first thing I could see was Walt sitting on the floor, disbelief and retaliation at war on his face.

He came up adroitly for a big man, snarling "I won't miss this time," and I moved up smartly to intercept him.

Again I was too late. This time though I saw "sompsing" (as Schmeling said in watching films of Joe Louis before their first bout), an incredible thing and one that told me that big Walt hadn't slipped the first time out. As Walt hooked a high and powerful right fist, Jim lithely turned into a pa-kua single palm change. The fist missed, Jim wrapped up the arm, scooped Walt's right foot, and there he was, again on his butt.

As I started to comment on the pa-kua, Jim asked incongruously, "What do you regard as Ethel Waters' best number?"

He sounded as calm as he looked. I tried to keep up with his incredible style, saying "I sort of like 'I Just Couldn't Take It Baby' best."

Fancher was having a helluva time. He couldn't figure it. He wasn't hurt, but he couldn't score. This inflamed him. And he was durable. Up he came, but as I moved toward him Jim said gently, "You get the next one."

It ought to have been choreographed. Walt swung a big boot that could've kicked out a wall at Jim who moved a fraction of an inch, the boot missed, and—snap—Jim grabbed his tibia, swung in, scooped the foot, and down the big guy went again. This time his big head rapped the wall smartly and he stayed down. He was one with Nineveh and Tyre.

Midway through this maneuver, Jim looked at me and shook his head. "I dunno; I favor 'Am I Blue'."

Not to be outdone on being fairly savoir, I retorted, "Our first disagreement. All I'll say is go back and listen to her final phrasing of 'I Just Couldn't Take It Baby', where she laughs huskily and says 'I can't get enough' and you'll see what sold me."

Jim had said I'd get the next one. He lied. But it wasn't his fault. From behind him a demon shouted "I wants you like a sow wants slops!" and out came Junior Fancher. Junior was a baby—a baby locomotive. Actually, he was small: he couldn't have been more than 225 pounds. And now Junior wanted to play trains, he had steam up, the pistons driving, and, boom, he piled into Jim. Almost. But either Junior's *kime* (focus) was awry, or Jim moved astoundingly quick.

The next thing I saw, Jim moved into Chang Chao-tung's famous "Monkey Offers Peach," deflected Junior's two hands with it and as Junior's momentum brought his body close, Jim brought up his two hands under his chin and drove them astride Junior's carotids. But gently. And then, holding his neck, Jim pivoted and drove Junior into the wall, which quieted him some.

It was neatly done and there was a pause in the proceedings. I asked Jim, "Who do you regard as the greatest guitar?"

"Easy," he said, "Eddie Lang. Many say Charlie Christian, but they confuse technology with art. Charlie revolutionized jazz guitar by plugging into an amplifier on the Benny Goodman bandstand in the thirties. Thereafter you had players more fascinated with the potential of electricity than with music."

"Right on! How about violin—Joe Venuti or Stuff Smith?"

We were interrupted at that point by Fred, a stranger to ethics, who yelled and attacked from what he thought was Jim's rear. By then I was a bit numb but still with it enough to see Jim adroitly turn and outward block with his right foot the size 12 boot Fred fetched up toward his groin and, with his foot still off the floor, simultaneously cut down with his left palm in Chang Chao-tung's famed "Yellow Dragon offers a Melon" to stop his incoming fist. It broke Fred's arm—and his will.

Then Jim looked at me and said, "Venuti."

We were running out of complainants. But yonder came Luke, no saint, with some choice epithets and a pair of pretty fast hands for a man of his bulk. Jim still had an arrow or two in his quiver. He did the Pa-kua double palm change on Luke quicker than you can say "finished", wrapped him up and

*Monkey Offers Peach to Junior Fancher*

sped him into the wall. That wall was like a giant fist, and while it didn't knock Luke out, it left him mumbling incoherently. He sat down, his eyes vacant with the used-up look of the dead.

That about did it. Phil was left, but he walked on up to Jim like he hadn't a care in the world. In fact he had the friendliest smile you ever saw on his face. Maybe because he was slender, I expected him to be the worst, and so I looked for him to have something coming soon. But surprisingly he walked right up to Jim and put out his hand, saying:

"Stranger, you won't believe this, but those boys needed that."

Jim smiled and shook his hand, "S'all right," he murmured.

No getting around it: the guy was cool. You'd watch for him to go past Jim's shake hand maybe, or for him to cross his left over the hands while they were shook. But not right after they stopped.

But that's what he did. He put his left hand in his pocket while he dug the right in the shortest most exquisite punch ever at Jim.

The thing was a gotcha all the way—but it got gobbled. I saw what it was. *Heng,* the "mother" fist of hsing-i boxing. No one else did, though.

All they saw was Phil flipped completely off the floor and into the wall and back onto the floor—unconscious. Unconscious? Maybe dead.

"Sorry boys," Jim said to the resting Fanchers, "had to hurt him a bit, he got too close. But he's tough, he'll be O.K. Just get him and yourselves out of here."

And they went. They had not been beaten so much as educated. Physically, they could show hardly a bruise. In the end they took their defeat and, though they weren't reconciled to it, they walked out more full of wonderment than revenge. No one went home for a gun—none of that kind of thing. They might say it was a "sleight" or trick, but if it was it was a good one and they'd never bother old Uncle Herman again.

As for ourselves, we sat there at a table with one of its legs hanging on for dear life. And in that denuded forest of upside-down tables and chairs we were kings.

But we reigned benevolently. It is harder to be a good winner than loser, but we did OK. We ordered hamburgers, and I began to talk.

I didn't mince words. "Jim you're some kind of reptile. Why didn't you tell me you could fight?"

He smiled warmly. "You didn't ask. And it wasn't fighting. It was more like getting out of the way of trucks on the Pennsylvania Turnpike."

I laughed. "Yeah, they didn't have a chance—you outnumbered them!"

He unbent a little. "Did you recognize it?"

"Hell, man, you may have me on old songs and you certainly hogged the limelight here tonight, but please leave me some dignity. That, old buddy, was classical pa-kua done rather well."

"Whose?" he bore in.

"Well, damned if it wasn't Chang Chao-tung's, one of China's greatest in a vintage period, but how the hell did a Nebraska farm boy learn it?"

Then he told me. His father had been in Peking on a farm exchange in 1922, met Chang, and stayed on for eight years studying pa-kua full time.

"He learned some hsing-i too, didn't he?" I asked.

He laughed again. "John, you may be lousy on songs but you know your boxing. You saw the *heng-ch'uan,* eh?"

"Yep, and it was a good choice. That Phil was dangerous."

"Not really," he said, "my dad always warned me never to let a man in close unless I was ready to go either way with *heng.*"

"It was the best I ever saw," I said.

"Thanks," he said, "but you should have seen my dad's."

The words were a valentine, alive with love. It is truly said, giants envy their fathers; only pygmies their sons.

Phil's hand had brushed the pen from his pocket and it lay now on the table. Jim picked it up. "Dad's old pen," he said, "A Parker Big Red from the 20's. We spoke earlier of style going out of American life. A case in point. Know how they advertised this back then?"

I shook my head.

"'It rivals the beauty of the scarlet tanager.'"

"Migod, that *was* style," I enthused.

The blonde brought the hamburgers, big and meaty, not the cardboard kind you get on a plastic dish most other places now in the good old U.S. of A. Before he took a bite, though, Jim surveyed the destruction in the room, the bartender and waitress—so shocked that they had suddenly become courteous—and mused: "This is the way the world ends—not with a bang but a wimpy."

# XI

# MAN VERSUS ANIMAL

*"Yer jest better leave that dog erlone. He's
mighty hard to whip, an' when he's whipped he
ain't but half whipped."*
—Eugene Rhodes

Compared to the animal kingdom, man is pretty puny. An ant can carry 20 times his own weight and a flea can jump 120 times its own length. A boxer's fist can reach 40 m.p.h. in the last few inches of travel but the gaff of a fighting cock is too quick for an ordinary camera to catch, and can go one-half inch into seasoned oak board. But don't believe the nonsense about a snake striking like lightning. A cobra at his speediest hits at 16 m.p.h. This relative slowness is what permits a mongoose to toy with him. Man can sprint for a limited time at 24 m.p.h.; a cheetah can go much longer at 70 m.p.h. A lion can kill game in less than a half-second and a sparrow hawk can swoop over a pond and pick off a swimming moorhen without a splash. The mantis strikes with such ferocity that even J. Henri Fabre, the naturalist, confessed to being startled witless each time he saw it. And they'll eat anything—including humming birds. The female mantis even devours the male during intercourse!

Some animals are so fast they can dodge bullets. A rifle bullet travels 40 yards in one-twentieth of a second, but weasels are able to dodge it. The loon is best at it. I knew a chap who shot seven times at one with a rifle, and the darned loon crash-dived away from each shot. In overall physical endurance the dolphin has it all over us, and some scientists say his brain power is on a par with ours also. His untiring agility in the water is equivalent to a man running to the top of Mt. Everest at 30 m.p.h. without stopping!

The fighting instinct is strong in animals. The clumsy, apparently almost blind, mole is as ferocious as a tiger; all the shrews' combats are to the death; and the kick of a hare can kill a polecat. One of the toughest is the pheasant who will easily dispatch the agile gamecock (as long as the latter isn't fitted out with metal spurs). The Arctic weasel has an ingeniously lithe body which can climb the highest trees, burrow into the deepest holes, and swim like a fish. And always after a meal. The only thing this creature can't do is fly. Maybe tougher though, is the water shrew, which can kill a fish 60 times heavier than himself by biting out its eyes and brain. This is roughly equivalent to a man killing an elephant barehanded.

The ruthless fighter who "knows no fear" does not get very far, says the world-famed biologist N. Tinbergen. The nine-foot-long Indian tiger will fight any animal in the world and—though he has no great desire for them—killed 1,000 or so Indians a year in the 1930's. But this king killer also fears something: he flees from the Indian *dhole* (wild dog) which hunts in large packs. Fear perhaps provides life a certain resonance.

Security in numbers works pretty well. The Cape hunting dogs travel in packs and are mean critters: the mother often kills her young, and the pack has a designated killer for the more sanguine jobs. But even numbers doesn't always do the trick. Baboons will gang up on a leopard, but never a lion.

Richard Jeffries, the English nature mystic, lauded men as being physically superior to animals. I have never understood how so consummate a naturalist could make such an error. Granted, the English countryside he knew was bereft of larger fang-and-claw species, but he had only to watch the agility of the red ant, the rapacious efficiency of the mantis, and the durability of the common cockroach to see the falsity of his contention. He cites a man who swam the channel—fish do it all the time. No, I think Jefferies was idealizing man as he might be spiritually, rather than what he really is physically.

Moreover, I know of no training short of weapons skill that will permit a man to defeat most wild animals. Not even with his teeth. A New Zealander, Dr. Ronald Every, believes that man defended himself for 12 million years primarily with his teeth. At that point he began to develop tools. Dr. Every says in effect that a man's teeth can be lethal and that evolution has provided him with built-in controls inhibiting their use in human combat. He cites as significant the fact that females and infants bit much more frequently when fighting than does the more powerful male. This is arguable. Females and infants may bite because they lack the powerful distance weapons, the fists, that the male has. But a man wanting to bite has to incur punishment from these weapons in order to get close. A man, unless he comes from Transylvania, has no fangs, only puny little pearlies. It's a cinch bet that Americans who cannot tear through cooked meat (of which we eat far too much) with their incisors and depend instead on dear old peristalsis, are going to have tough chewing on a neck wet with sweat. Now if you really want to compete on bites, listen. The jaws of an eight-foot long shark recently measured on a special instrument were found to exert a force of *20 tons per square inch.* In dental terms, that's an overbite!

Occasionally one reads of a man besting an animal, but it's best to stay skeptical. Just today I heard of a jock at some university panty-raid who, confronted by a large German shepherd, grabbed the animal's jaws and ripped his head apart. This is silly. If I had been told that the guy clamped the dog's jaws together and held them (he'd need a couple of confederates to hold the dog's body), I could go along with the story. But these dogs have enormous "bite" power in their jaws—far, far too much for even the legendary strongman, Louis Cyr, to rip them apart.

Take the bear. Everyone knows someone who's outwrestled one. Don't you believe it. The bear is the best wrestler among animals. According to the old folk saying, "He has the intellect of one, the strength of nine men." Only when he is tamed can he be defeated by a man.

What saves man is his magnificent mind. It is far faster than his body. In a crisis, the mind leisurely assays the situation, relates, and remembers. There is an old story that when Battling Munroe was kayoed by Sam Langford, an entire novel he had once read unfolded itself in his subconscious mind during the ten seconds of the count. I love this story and I believe in time distortion, but I don't believe it because of its central point. It asks you to believe that Battling Munroe had once read a novel.

Man's mind and that beautiful prehensile thumb let him make weapons that compensated for his lack of talons, hoofs, venom, and his slow speed. And his weapons ultimately have unleashed the power to destroy that environment—and himself with it.

But before he leaves the stage, man seems intent on getting his kicks from exploiting, teasing, injuring, and killing the animals he now has no need to fear. Without getting up on my soapbox, I must say I am against all needless killing of animals. I regard "sport" hunting as hurting the killer, man, as much as the animal victim.

Just as I believe one should not interfere with two consenting adults in the act of intercourse—"as long as it doesn't frighten the horses," as Lady Astor put it—I also think that two men who wish to fight should be permitted to do so. This presupposes that they are not manipulated into it by money, media, managers, or madness. I draw the line, however, on animals being taught to fight by men.

Take dog fighting, currently growing in popularity in America. Some of the sick among us force Staffordshire terriers and other dogs to fight, often to the death. These fights last from a half-hour to 2½ hours and the poor winner envies the dead loser. This is a throwback to Merrie Old England in the seventeenth century when dogs were bred and taught to fight and die. A real time to be alive. As a man, not a dog or bull. During this period a bull couldn't be killed without first baiting it to improve the meat. Courage was everything: a game dog was life's dearest possession. He had to be game because he fought under the most severe rules imaginable. He had to cross the pit and fight or be declared the loser. Breeding was always with a view to tactics: the bulldog had a vice-like bite but was too slow. So they crossed him with a white terrier and the synthesis was no longer a dog but an animal that would die rather than take a backward step.

It was ridiculous and got more so. Soon they had dogs competing to kill rats in a pit. Inevitably came the day a man went into the pit, hands tied in back of him, to try and outdo the dogs at rat-killing. Captain L. Fitz-Bernard in *Fighting Sports* writes that the man was really quick but not the equal of the better dogs. And men could be induced to go in using only their fists against a bull-dog. The men invariably won, but they were sorry messes afterwards.

Cockfighting is even worse, because here men arm the poor birds they make fight. St. Augustine, it is said, approved of cockfighting because "a higher being was regulating all they did." I'll never be a saint: to me cock-fighting is ignoble man regulating the short unsweet passage from life to death of these birds.

The Chinese have conducted cricket matches since the Sung Dynasty. They're still held in Macau with bets ranging from three cents to $40. Only males fight and they do it in a 10 by 20-inch ring. Strong mandibles either kill or incapacitate one of the fighters. The only solace to this bestiality is that the males are permitted to mate the night before a match. A boxer in Hong Kong once wanted to learn boxing from me, but when I found he regularly attended these things I refused, telling him frankly that he didn't have the requisite character for me to teach him. He was interested in death. Correct boxing is only interested in life.

Perhaps the most abominable monument to man's bestiality is bull-fighting. C. M. Bowra, the authority on Greece, once defined the epic hero as "He who pursues honor through risk." But there's precious little risk to bull-fighting, and no honor. It is simply not honorable first to make a bull mad and then kill him. Or to kill him in a game not of his own choosing where the odds are carefully stacked against him. For he is never allowed to fight twice—he learns too quickly—and the second time the odds would change drastically in his favor. The matador, Diego Bardon, turned in his cape and sword a few years back in Madrid, saying: "The saddest thing about it is that the fighting bulls are never mated and it is doubly cruel that they should die and die before they have had a chance to make love." A man, friends, a man.

I can't understand the sickness that goes into these wretched pursuits. But then, I'm stupid: I never understood how a nation like America, reared on fair play, with more churches than taverns, and more collge graduates than old drunks could have perpetrated the villainy it did in Vietnam.

To summarize: man is a weakling in the animal kingdom. His natural weapons are pitiable. But God graced him with a mind and, rumor hath it, an ethical sense. Cleveland Amory wrote: "Giraffes don't use their forefeet, with which they can kill lions, on other giraffes. Rattlesnakes fight each other without using their deadly venom. Skunks squirt their secretion at predators, not at other skunks. Some day man, too, will renounce nuclear and biological weaponry. Then at least we can say he has the brains of a giraffe, the sense of a rattlesnake, and the decency of a skunk."

Clearly man has misused his mind with the result that animals suffer and, along with them, ironically, the human animal. Man's ethical sense is guttering out like an old candle, extinguishing not only his flame but the one quality that could redeem him—his shame.

# XII

# CHANG SAN-FENG LIVES!

*"We wanted Li Wing
But we winged Willie Wong,
A sad but excusable
Slip of the tong."*

—Keith Preston

Chang San-feng, the traditional founder of t'ai-chi, was called La T'a (dirty fellow). He had only one set of clothes. He seldom spoke but when he did it was always on the classics and then the words came like a torrent. Similarly, he would not eat for months and then, when he did, would eat bushels. When he was asked where his food went he said, "The ghosts eat it!" In winter he slept in the snow.

In 1965 I heard of a fellow named Lu who had made it his lifework to follow Chang in nearly every particular, hoping thereby to come by the original t'ai-chi, the pure method without the barnacles. According to my source, whom I'll call Tom Phillips, this Lu lived out beyond 110th and Broadway on the West side of Manhattan Island, that place egregiously misnamed "fun city." He was Chinese, but looked more Japanese. His landlady said he'd lived there since World War II. He may have come from China on a freighter and jumped ship, because three Chinese aliens were picked up at the same apartment in the fifties on a day when Lu mysteriously disappeared. Although he was never gone from his room for long periods, had no job, and never received so much as a postcard, the day the Feds came by scouring the pads and picked up the three aliens Lu was gone, as he was on subsequent occasions when they came. Some of this story came from Phillips; a lot came from the landlady, who even at sixty would do anything for money. Lu's schedule was precise and consistent. At 6:30 a.m. and 11 p.m. each day he left his room for a half-hour walk. The rest of the time he remained in his room.

There were many curious things about the man. He looked 60 in 1950 and 50 when I saw him in 1965. Although straight, he looked bent, and he was dirty as hell. He moved awkwardly, shambling along, exhibiting alacrity only to jump obsequiously out of the way of people. In fact, he was so servile, Gandhi would have knocked him down and found pleasure in it.* He spoke little, using "huh" to do service for his oral needs.

This worked well because—and here's the kicker—he had no needs. He almost never ate out or bought anything. Though he had a hotplate in his room, the landlady said that there was no evidence that it had ever been used nor was there even a crumb of food found there. The flats were continually being renovated and at least twice during the years Lu had been shifted to another room while his was being upgraded to an almost livable condition.

He never had a visitor and didn't encourage talk. He read nothing. Or almost nothing. On two occasions, occurring in consecutive years at Chinese New Year in February, he is known to have eaten at a nondescript Chinese restaurant. Phillips interviewed the young waiter there and verified that the man involved was Lu. The waiter thought but couldn't be sure that the same man had eaten—at New Years, again—a couple of years before the first incident that left such an indelible mark on the waiter. On that occasion Lu, dirty and unkempt, was almost not seated because of his appearance. But the owner, feeling charitable during the holidays, relented and, even though it looked like a gratis meal, he told the young waiter to serve the man. Well they served him . . . and kept serving him.

After the first hour of systematic and wholesale devouring of a pot of noodles, the old man had ordered an encore. The owner flushed his good intentions down the spiritual drain, and moved in to reject the order. Then it was that Lu brought forth from his own wrinkled brown trousers a roll of greenbacks that would stuff a Wall Street banker. The owner gulped and, to cover his retreat, suggested that maybe a change to rice would add variety to the fare. Lu scarcely stopped slurping the noodles but grunted out, "Rice is for southern talkers:  you hit a rice-eater in the belly and it's the end of him." Well, the owner, being a burly Cantonese and like most Chinese cooks fancying himself a boxer, almost fetched Lu one up alongside the jaw, but his commercial instinct (keep this guy eating) and his curiosity (how much is he

*Baudelaire, the French poet, was once accosted by a beggar who looked so servile it offended the poet and he insulted the man. Forthwith the man knocked him to the pavement. Baudelaire got up and observed that whereas before they had had no proper relationship, now that one had been established he would be pleased to share his purse with him.

*A Transformed Lu Comes for His Book*

going to eat?) got the better of him. He kept the noodles coming. All told, Lu logged five hours on that consumption function and the bill came to $84.00. That is a helluva lot of noodles. He left a $25 tip by the plate.

During his last half hour in the restaurant, Lu read from a small book, which he kept turned away from the darting eyes of the waiters. And after he was gone, the young waiter found the book—it was really only a manuscript stapled together. Saying nothing to his fellows, the waiter took a break, beat it for the street, and walked hurriedly to Riverside Park, where he latched onto a bench. Ensconced there, he perused the book. It was in classical Chinese and the kid had a slow go with it. But in the short time he had it, he made out that it was a secret teaching of Chang San-feng having to do with the respiratory, meditative, and dietary aspects of boxing. I say short time, because within five minutes the waiter looked up and saw a man big and tall and altogether awesome striding toward him. He did a Jimmy Cagney double-take and recognized in this approaching behemoth the dirt and squalor of old man Lu.

The youngster fairly quaked. He stuck the book out for the man to take. Lu took it without a word and was gone, seeming almost to disappear—but fear may have contributed to this perception of the waiter.

Well, the next year Lu returned to the restaurant and, though served by the same waiter, appeared not to recognize him. This time he ate over $100 worth of noodles (with inflation, this may not have indicated a real increase in consumption), perused his book, left a $50 tip, and as he had the year before left a shocked and stunned bunch when he left. That time, however, he didn't leave his book.

Phillips found four other Chinese restaurants who remembered the enormous gustatory feats of an old man on their premises at different New Years. From this I speculate that Lu perhaps ate that one meal a year, and that sufficed. By itself, however, this isn't unique. I met years before a nun in Chang-sha and a yogi in Amritsar who were kept under constant surveillance. If they ever ate a morsel it escaped the eyes of their vigilant watchers.

But what it does show is that Lu was literally reliving the life of Chang San-feng. Add to this, he appeared to get younger each year, his hair became full and jet black, and his face had nary a wrinkle. One could say that Lu was succeeding.

Except for one thing: did this ascetic existence help in any way his boxing? Phillips, who had served 15 years in police work, uncovered some astonishing facts in this regard. Now, unsolved crimes in New York City are no rarity. The precinct records are full of them. But, since the fifties, street crime in this area is far below other areas. And it shouldn't be, housing as it does students and all manner of people. In the fifties police started finding batches of two or three men badly beaten on the streets in the area. One night in 1953 they found six.

The puzzling thing about these victims was that they themselves were criminals or small-time muggers. The police, without examining the pattern (who was it who said that the New York police force was the best money could buy?), put it down as gang warfare. But the gangs themselves were puzzled, and the beaten who didn't make it to the pokey kept an embarrassed silence.

Years later Phillips ran a couple of these birds down and bought the truth from them. Both told how they with several friends had jumped an old man to divest him of his wallet and, if he complained, his life. The next thing they knew they were in the criminal ward at a nearby hospital. What had they remembered about his tactics? "Eerie, it was," one said. "He didn't do much; just seemed to touch everyone like he was playing tag. Trouble was, it made everyone fall down."

Sounds like Chang San-feng, doesn't it? Though Lu probably never

*Lu Descends on a Phantom Elevator*

accumulated the hundred men that Chang beat in one fight in old China, he seems to have made that section of New York City safer.

Anyhow in 1965, after talking to Phillips, I went up there and took a room in the same place and bought me an earful of the old landlady. The room I rented was pretty drab.

And I saw Lu—just once. The elevator wasn't working one evening, so I walked from the fourth floor down, meeting no one on the stairs. The lobby was empty as I came down but just then the elevator door opened and Lu walked off it, slightly ahead of me. I caught up with him and held the door open for him, and murmured "Mr. Lu." He wasn't a bit servile, smiled sweetly at me, said "Mr. Gilbey," and went out into the night. I guess. For half-way through the door he no longer was there. I felt foolish holding the door for apparently no one, glided through it, and looked up and down the street. Need I say? He had vanished.

I went back in and rousted out the landlady. It was 11:05 p.m. She thought I was drunk at first when I asked about the elevator.

"That damned thing hasn't worked for two days," she said. I looked it over, sure enough, it was inoperative; the main cable had disintegrated from lack of maintenance. Why was I interested? she queried.

I told her I thought I saw Lu come off it. Impossible, she said, he never uses the elevator. Likes to walk the stairs? I asked. She paused, looked funny, and said, "Come to think of it, I've never seen him come down the stairs either." So here is a man living on the sixth floor who passes through the lobby once each day and night, pays his rent there, but is never seen descending. A hard guy to get a purchase on. But I had one more arrow: his consistency. I bade the landlady goodnight and waited in the lobby. Sure enough, at 11:30 the door opened and no one came in—or should I say Lu came in? The door opened outward onto the street, hence the wind couldn't have done it. I know it was Lu because the damned door did it again at 6:30 and 7:00 next morning as I stood there.

As far as I know Lu still lives up there—he was still paying rent in 1977. And probably will as long as brainless muggers jump lonely old men on Manhattan's dark streets.

# XIII

# THE MASTER OF
# APPLIED COWARDICE

*"After all, th' only ole, reliable,*
*safe an' sane sport is croquet."*
—Anonymous

A Harvard player in the 1894 football game with Yale landed a right cross to the immortal jaw of Yale's Frank Hinkey. "My friend," said Hinkey, "if you hit me another like that you'll break your hand."

Hinkey was tough but he wasn't indestructible. What the vignette shows is grand *panache,*\* or to put it more plainly, *style.* You remember how Cyrano spouted poetry in the process of undoing a bad "un". That was *panache.* This flair isn't restricted to class: I've seen farmers exhibit it as often and as easily as college men.

But one of the best at all three—fighting, poetry, and *panache*—was a college man, a professor named Jed Connor. I met Jed years ago at a poetry congress in Louisville, home of beautiful horses, fast women, and Kentucky bourbon, only one of which I'd sell much of my soul for. I had been told about Jed by Bill Paul, who had taught him his course in "applied cowardice."

Let me explain. The first and last lesson of any worthwhile martial art is the avoidance of fighting. It is not enough simply to espouse this as an ethic. It has to be taught . . . and learned. And just as assiduously as the more offensive mechanics.

Bill Paul, former west coast judo champ, actually has created and taught such a course in recent years. In the course Bill teaches a full-range of aspects,

---

\*Corneille was the French writer who put *panache* into the language. In the same way Chinese warrior-nobles had graciously offered 2,000 years earlier, a French officer at Fontenoy says to officers of King George II: "You gentlemen may fire first." That is *panache.*

such as: graceful exits, individuation, appeals to ego, ego salvage, the balance of power, and the possibilities of humor. Then, using the Asian martial arts as a base, Bill teaches the tyro functional non-violent defense techniques of posture, movement, recovery, disengagement, and escape. (Rumor hath it that Bill perfected these techniques from field experience in peace marches in which Hell's Angels—ever on the wrong side—were wont to assault the passive. But I understand that at that time Bill didn't have a good grasp of the ideas he later developed—and often cheated.)

The course is not easy. Peace is always harder than war. It is rigorous; he tosses his pupils into simulated combat with never a backward glance. In controlled situations, Bill would teach an offensive karate group and a defensive "cowardice" group separately for a semester and then have them compete. The result was always the same—the defensive group won.

Bill told me that Jed, a former golden glove champ and judo 3-dan, was his best student, a guy with moxie, and a good poet to boot. So I wrote and shook hands with Jed by letter, and the first chance I got I went on down to Caintuck. He invited me out to his ramshackle abode where I met his deep-eyed wife, Sarah, and his three kids.

I "relished verse" and had published some, but he was a real poet. And he had comfortable chairs.

"Poetry," he started, "is the smile on the face of truth. The smile says I will be here or someplace very like here when the mountains are flat.

"Poetry is life just as fighting is life. And just as a good poem is never completed, only abandoned, so fighting is a never-ending process. No one was ever a perfect fighter. 'The unflawed pot,' you know."

While discussing poetry, we were eating home-made donuts (what the cowboys used to call "bear find") and drinking superb coffee. Ah, coffee, it's getting a bad name these days. We can spend $300 billion for defense during detente but we come down hard on the evils of the black stuff. Why? Because it will kill you. Sure, but the things we eat and the air we breathe and the thoughts we think do that just as rapidly.

Voltaire drank 50 cups a day and Balzac, 40. Talleyrand liked it "Black as the devil, hot as hell, pure as an angel, and sweet as love."

Now, I don't drink much, a cup or two a day. Jamaican Blue Mountain when I can get it, otherwise Kona, Yunnan, or Columbian will do. I know most people abuse it by overdrinking and by swallowing the ersatz instant bilge. It gives you pause to watch some folks sit for 20 minutes over a cup of instant coffee.

Nope. Coffee is getting a bad rap. There comes a time when it is incomparable, a time caught beautifully by J. Frank Dobie: "I want to sit down with some old rawhide and listen to him blow his coffee, listen to him make a kind of solemn-joyful noise unto the Lord, an unconscious characterizing expressive of the mighty response of his whole body to coffee . . ."

But poetry wasn't the end of Jed. He shared my interest in the martial and my abhorrence of modern war. We might have been different in another time. But World War I ended chivalry. Before that, one had conducted and been part of a relationship with the enemy. Afterwards, technology alienated every soldier from the actions he himself took.

Jed also liked chess and was a pretty fair hand at it, but was smart enough not to take it seriously. "Most great chess players are mad. Did you ever hear of Steinitz?" he asked.

"Sure, wasn't he the one so all-fired deluded he thought he could move the pieces without touching them?"

"Right, he was a pip. Once challenged God, offering him pawn and move. Question is: does chess drive people like him crackers or is there something about chess that draws wacky people? I don't know."

"I remember Marcel Duchamp writing that chess was important because it had absolutely no social function."

"Keerect. And Chesterton more than once urged doing the meaningless, the thing with no utility in life as a good path. So he'd agree with Duchamp. But I'm not sure that this non-utility had anything to do with making chessmasters mad. On the contrary. To do something for its own sake apart from any accruing utility strikes me as something that would drive a man sane, not crazy."

But most of the time we spent on what turned out to be a too-short weekend we talked about his brand of fighting or, more concretely, non-fighting. Bill Paul had demonstrated the system and had touched a sympathetic chord in me. I first gave Jed some of my views on it.

Avoidance should not be construed as cowardice. In this context I am reminded of a delicious story by Bertold Brecht. A town is conquered by vandals and the high priest's home taken over by the commander. He brusquely tells the priest: "You will clean my house, prepare my food, and cater to my every wish. You will be my slave. Do you consent?" Without answering, the priest sets about scrubbing the floor and performing other menial jobs. He serves the commander for ten years, at the end of which the Vandal dies and his army is overthrown. The priest buries him; then spits on the grave and answers, "No."

The art of any real fighting system is in never having to use what you've learned. Thus, it is aimed at you and no one else. The old phrase "judo teaches you to run with confidence" still rings with the profound. I've always—well, almost always—believed and practiced this.

Once years ago in Chicago I went into a small Chinese grocery with a young man who was trying to pump me for "wisdom." As I entered the store, I must have brushed too close to a behemoth in a World War II khaki coat. I was selecting some groceries when the young man approached and from the side of his mouth told me that the big guy had taken offense at me and that I should watch out. As I took my purchases to the front counter, I looked khaki over with peripheral vision. He was 6'1", 220 pounds, aged 48 or thereabouts. And pretty well soused.

I didn't look directly at him for the same reason one doesn't look a snarling, threatening dog in the eye—the look becomes a challenge. But I kept part of an eye on him and my ears tuned toward him. The little Chinese owner must have noticed because he swiped his cleaver down meaningfully near my groceries. Khaki shuffled out the door.

As I was paying, the young man again came over, saying "He's waiting outside." In our previous discussion I had tried to make the point that the greatest fighting skill exists in never using that skill. Now I tested the youngster.

"Do you really want to see some sophisticated boxing?" I asked him.

He salivated like What's-His-Name's dogs. "I sure would."

"O.K. then watch," I told him. Then turning to the little grocer, "Do you have a back door?"

He did, showed it to us, and we exited without incident. Outside, I could see the boy was disappointed.

"What good," I asked him, "would it do to belabor a poor drunk? All it would do is increase the violence in the world by meeting his alcohol-induced hate with your own. It would certainly not add to one's knowledge of boxing."

He pretended to believe—but I don't think he did. Conditioned by a desperately confused and violent culture, he saw the best solutions as sanguine ones.

We might remember the story of the old jujutsu master whose *dojo* was in the midst of a small wood. A little path led to his 18-mat *dojo*. On the narrow path one day someone had tethered a demented jackass. As the first student going to practice approached the animal, it lashed out with a foot, breaking his leg. He started to crawl home, but then, wondering how the others would fare, he hid in the bushes to watch. Soon another student approached the animal but, being more skillful than the first, he was able to turn slightly and the kick only shattered his kneecap. He too jumped in the bushes to monitor developments. The best *jujutsuka* came along shortly, walked right up to the animal, sensed something, and did a beautiful turn and the kick missed him entirely. Afterwards he hid in the bushes to see how the old master would handle the mad beast. Finally the old man came along the path, decrepit and full of years but withal graceful. As he approached the jackass he paused, walked around the other side of him, and proceeded down the path. His jujutsu art was avoidance.

Then it was Jed's turn, sitting there in that rumpled suit: "It is a law of nature that if a species' weapons are not dangerous, the inhibitory mechanism is absent. This may be one of the reasons man is so violent: in comparison with most animals his weapons are extremely ineffectual. Whereas snakes and bears wrestle, central European sand lizards take turns biting each other without breaking the skin, and a wolf beaten in a tussle offers his throat to another, these things inhibit use of lethal weapons. But man's natural weapons are not lethal. There is no code restricting the use of the rudimentary weapons he has.

"A part of nature's inhibitory mechanism is to give the defeated room to escape. If he is caged with the victor, death may ensue. Running room is necessary. If, for example, monkeys, rats, and hamsters are prevented from flight, death is frequent.

"In Bill's system, which I've adapted to my own boxing and judo, we make that running room and use it to its fullest. We become geniuses of the fast get-away. This makes our system the most self-defensive in the catalog. Now most Asian fighting arts claim that they are self-defensive and never, never aggressive.

"And some truly are. T'ai-chi, correctly taught, doesn't even relate function to posture. And there is an Okinawan style of karate, *Shuri-no-te,* the art-of-not-fighting, which is premised on the sane notion that walking away is better than causing harm to someone who is apparently out of harmony with himself, nature, or his fellow beings. And there are a few judo teachers who teach the art as it was first created by Jigoro Kano: enlightened jacketed wrestling.

"But practice doesn't live up to theory. The result is that too many martial art types can hardly wait for a chance to vent their spleen and knuckles on some poor unoffending fighter. Gichin Funakoshi, the great Okinawan karate expert, really believed in an ethic, however. In fact, his motto was *karate ni sent naski* (karate has no offense). But in his autobiography he acknowledged how quickly many students departed from the ideal.

"Our method is systematic and scientific. And psychologically sound. It is not trickery. You know the assassin bug?"

I didn't.

"Well, when it is attacked by an ant, it releases a fluid from its abdomen and offers it to the ant. The ant likes the stuff and munches it so greedily that he fails to notice the bug's forelegs slowly encircling its neck."

"Shades of the *thugee*," I put in.

"Right," said he. "While that kind of trickery may touch a poetic impulse, it is really a cheap shot, oblique rather than direct violence. As devious as it is imaginative, but essentially as violent as violence. Our system isn't like that. It is simply one of educated movement shorn of deceit.

"The three important things are time, distance, and exposure. All are crucial. The attacker will attempt to make his move as rapidly across as short a distance with as little exposure as possible. Your job is to extend all these factors.

"Let's start with the preliminaries, which are as vital here as they are in love. The way you stand and act may actually cause an attack. So try to stand out of an opponent's immediate zone—defined as his height's distance away from him. And stand at a diagonal to him. If you stand frontal, he may regard it as threatening. Your hands obviously should not be clenched or on your hips or even crossed in front of your chest. Any of these he may perceive as threatening. He may even be alarmed by hands held in back of you. So hold them open in full sight.

"Now, the typology of the attacker is that in a crisis (or what he views as one) he takes on tunnel vision; his focus is limited to a narrow strip immediately ahead of him. Work to keep out of this tunnel. Try to avoid sharp angles in your stance. Have as loose and rounded an attitude as possible. Keeping out of his territory with just such an inoffensive posture and mien may be sufficient to preclude the attack. At a minimum, if he is adept in the art of premature self-defense, these precautions may prevent his suckering you.

"But maybe they won't. Then you go into your avoidance routine. If he does a two-hand choke on your throat, simply put the fingers of your left hand against his trachea and push off. This will bounce you away from him backwards.

"Or say he closes the distance, sets himself with his left foot forward and throws a right fist. This time, thrust against his chest with your left hand while kicking off backward. The rebound will let you avoid his fist easily. It is impossible for him to hit you if your thrust is timed right. And the thrust can be against his arm as well as his chest.

"Moving back is done by pushing off your front foot as you push off his body. It can be a chopping, rapid step as you take the front foot toward the rear, push off, and repeat. Or it can be a big floating sequence. It all depends on the attack itself. Accompanying the step, keep slapping out non-offensively with your hands at his eyes, all the while trying to get him to desist.

"The key, of course, is that you extend time, distance, and exposure by moving back. The thrust is not an attack—simply a means of propelling yourself back. Now as you move back, your hands are kept in a western boxing position and your feet don't cross.

"So he's missed. You've tried to talk him out of it as you've moved away from him. He probably didn't even notice your thrust. But he knows he's missed. He didn't get you quick and close. And he's been exposed. People who didn't notice the oral dispute now are aware of the physical. He's getting exposure and he feels foolish. So that may end it.

"Or it may not. He makes another approach, you leap back, and he has to take an extra step round the corner to confront you (this because of your diagonal stance). But he catches you and strikes again. Thrust and leap away. You can keep this up all day. But he can't. The factors have run out on him. In fact, Ray Lunny, the Stanford boxing coach, uses pretty much the same tactics and, past 50, will take on anyone without getting his hair mussed.

"The basic exercises in this method (hell, it's almost methodless; all it requires of the practitioner is extreme cowardice) are thrusting off a wall in such a way that the legs don't cross and are then ready for the next backward move. The rest is simply avoidance and your body can be trained to it by a lot of backward running and various sports. The thing is easy because it's natural. You already have the skill of hand and eye and leg coordination—it comes with a ballglove—all you have to do is adapt it to this system.

"The best preparation for this system is in wrestling and western boxing. These teach you good footwork and also show you how to be comfortable in close. But they also can give you an attacking tendency which could be fatal. So you've got to be selective in what you take from them.

"Handball is perhaps the best adjunctive sport for any system of combatives including this one. It is a fast game, requires rapid eyes, and the use of all body components. The feet are synchronized to brain and eye and must go in all directions, backwards as often as frontwards. The body is forced to play high as often as low. So it covers a whole range of effort. Tennis is much more limited."

The best example in western boxing of carrying this off with élan was Jimmy Wilde who at 100 pounds won the flyweight championship of the world and often boxed featherweights (126 pounds). Being so light, he obviously couldn't trade punches with many of the fighters he faced. Instead, he would invariably move to the rear, fending off the volleys as they came, blocking, slipping (taking the head laterally out of the path of incoming punches), ducking, and then countering. And, oh, he could counter! His knockout record was 56%, an astounding percentage against men who were so much bigger.

"But in the ring Wilde was much more constrained than a person in the street need be. We can run and try to hide. He couldn't.

"'Bicycle' Bob Pastor tried to against Louis," I put in. "He ran like a thief and survived the first ten rounds of the first fight, and the only way he got a rematch was to agree to a 20-round bout. Before that one Louis said 'He can run, but he can't hide.' He was right. He got Pastor in the eleventh round of the second go. Jeffries and Langford also had trouble with runners. Trying to catch one guy, Langford knocked him out—believe it or not!—by hitting him in the buttocks! Another guy, Jeffries knocked down with a right to the coccyx."

"Right. They had trouble, but they were still able to get their man because of the restricting ring. But we don't have that problem. Space is our ally and our antagonist's enemy."

"That's why I've found that one of the most necessary and effective ingredients of this method is running backward for two miles each day. This is hard, tedious, and boring work, but it is absolutely essential. My better boys I even have do wind sprints backwards, and there is one—Steve Kelley—who can do a 100 yards in under 17 seconds."

"Not as good as Bill 'Bojangles' Robinson's record," I said, "but he's gaining."

"If you can outrun your oncoming opponent then there is often no need to close with him. And, attacking takes more out of a man than defending. To the long distance and sprint ability going backward, I add the lateral move going either way. This gives us four avenues if you count going into the man— which we will do but only in a pinch. He can follow us down these dark mean streets but always, because he is reacting, he will be a shade behind. If he catches up we permutate him with shoves, slaps, and if necessary actual punches. Even here we first attempt evasion but if strikes or throws are required we use them—but only for temporary effect. The stress is always on movement."

I interrupted him here to praise the system. Most so-called new systems I had found came from men unable to stand the discipline of an orthodox method. The result was that most were as inefficient as a trombone player with TB.

But then I made a mild rebuttal of the system, saying, "You don't have to understand Werner Heisenberg's Theory of Indeterminacy to know that human knowledge is incomplete. Nothing is known for sure. Heisenberg concluded that it is tough enough to measure one aspect of a sitting duck precisely, but when motion is introduced, all bets are off. What the esteemed scientist didn't realize is that the indeterminacy or uncertainty of measurement applies even without the motion.

"It is commonly believed that a fighter must move; otherwise he is vulnerable to an attacker. It ain't necessarily so. Some Tibetan and Chinese master boxers stand very still and wait for the opponent's move, believing that *any* move the opponent makes provides an opening for a *riposte.* They use no fancy footwork and they hold their arms still. To them, most foot and arm maneuvers are more a function of a boxer's nervousness than of a strategy. Movement does several things, all bad: (1) it betrays nervousness, (2) it shows a posture that the attacker can utilize, and (3) it blocks the meridians, impedes blood and energy, and hampers breathing. In short, for the body to respond efficiently it cannot be a divided force. The energy that fells the attacker is whole-body energy, delivered in a flash.

"These masters must have sensed something else. Psychologist John Hughlings has recently noted that the human eye and its cerebral-anchor can stay focused on a static object for only a minute or so. After which some sort of adjustment is necessary. You blink—and even though this is done in one-fortieth of a second it's a big opening for some boxers—close your eyes, shake your head, etc., and then restart."

Jed shook his shaggy head. "I grant your thesis and proofs. But, John, your master boxer is not going to assault anyone. He's not the one this system has to deal with. We are dealing with hung-up crazies who want to pile on us like Ossa on Pelion. It all reduces to the pivotal proposition: 'If God had wanted us to fight, why did he give us legs?' "

The man who thinks he knows it all is a pain in the neck to those of us who really do. But Jed's rebound was resoundingly on the mark. It was true and made the system all the more pleasing.

"Your method then is so geared to rapid retreat, it wouldn't know how to be offensive?" I asked.

"Not quite," he answered. "You've heard of the Parthian Shot? Well, it got its name from the Parthians, a group of Persians who emigrated from Scythia to what is now Iran in the first century B.C. These Parthians were notorious for their method of warfare in which they would fake a pell-mell retreat when the first spear was hurled at them. Shortly thereafter though, they would wheel around and catch the over-anxiously pursuing enemy unawares with a quick, massive volley. That last and most effective shot is the Parthian Shot. And we're not above using it. It doesn't have to be a thing of beauty or a joy forever. Perfection can be death in the street. You don't need a clean throw or strike. All you need is a bump or half-trip; anything to make him stumble will suffice to let you extricate or, if you must, get yours in. But I stress we use it only in an emergency. Most of the time, we just run. *That* is our art."

# XIV

# PEACE, BROTHERS AND SISTERS, PEACE

*The Master, indeed, does not fight,*
*Therefore his inner life increases.*

—Lao-tze

Fighting is invariably violent but it needn't be cruel. There is something to be said for it when it is done sportively. But not much, even at this level. Why?

Because there is a better way of getting rid of inner tensions: other sports, reading, or good deeds will ease or eradicate these. If recourse to the physical is needed, then there is no better remedy than recreational wrestling or judo.

Nowadays, TV regales us with violence gone berserk. This has to have a powerful effect on us, none of it good. If ever there was a case for restraint, this is it. We continue to censor sex but violence is given carte blanche. The TV magnates hoist themselves on their own petard by arguing that there is no causal link between the abominations they show us and actual violence, that TV has no influence on us. Nonsense. If true, why do giant firms spend billions annually on commercials for just that purpose—to influence us to buy their products?

Each society has the criminals it deserves. The U.S. today has more criminals per capita than any nation has ever had. And more vicious criminals. Where did they come from? From society, from us. "We have met the enemy," said the late great Pogo, "and he is us."

Scientists have found that violence—particularly of the directed or state-directed type seen at My Lai—achieves the acme of cruelty when the victim is defenseless. This gives the perpetrator a "wholesome" feeling of omnipotence.

Until now, most of the cruelty inflicted has been of a directed or task-oriented kind. But more and more our personal violence has come to take on a gratuitously cruel pattern.

These words have added point because they come from one schooled from childhood in the science of efficient violence. And one who now sighs these words of *Psalm 22:*

> I am poured out like water, and all my bones are out of joint: my heart is like wax; it is melted in the midst of my bowels. My strength is dried up like a potsherd; and my tongue cleaveth to my jaws; and thou hast brought me to the dust of death.

Why does violence persist? First, because it is profitable for some to exploit interest in it. Like it or not, there is a deep craving for collision in us (Freud's death wish?) This can be sublimated in a hundred different ways, but many prefer the crude and cruel. Happily, the preference is usually for a vicarious type of experience. But if we enjoy it vicariously, it stands to reason we will aggress in some degree in our human relationships. This is the fact and the danger. Things tend to escalate and proliferate.

Religion can do little to alleviate the barbarism. It stopped trying long ago. Religion in the U.S. nowadays is pretty well summed up by a story my nephew told me. Down at his small college in Georgia they had a former green beret chaplain come in to talk. He was handsome and erect but had a funny look in his eyes as though he didn't quite trust you, the world, himself. Well my nephew thought he would get some sanguinary words on how God and the U.S. gave 'em hell in Vietnam, but nossir. This chaplain, an unreconstructed Baptist, lectured to those poor kids on how he had overcome the terrible sin of biting his fingernails! To sanction such an intellectually silly and morally abhorrent war, but to consign to eternal hellfire the chewers of fingernails cries out for intolerance.                                          .

A sweet fundamentalist lady whose 16-year old son was into kung fu and who read my first book and was reading Lao-tze and Confucius wrote me, worrying. Would these teachers harm her boy? I wrote her back that these sages wouldn't hurt him a bit since apparently Christ had made no impact on him. If He had, mama should have been writing me about the harm boxing might do him. This hadn't occurred to her. Back she came saying violence was human; we could do nothing about it. It comes with the territory.

Hogwash. You can take that nonsense and put it where the sun never shines. It's an old argument and some scientists buy it. Konrad Lorenz studied geese while the Nazi poison swirled around him and later rationalized his ostrich stance by saying that since evil was inbred there was nothing he *could* have done about it (the ineffable Jack Rosenberg of est would say that the victims were at fault—their *karma* invited incineration). Lionel Tiger and Robin Fox coupled this purported impulse to kill with the impulse to copulate. How silly: men are recruited and in various ways forced to kill in modern warfare. Have you heard of any who had to be forced to copulate?

Stuart Piggott in his seminal *Ancient Europe* writes, "One of man's most deeply seated and most cherished needs is for aggression . . . against his fellow man." Are we genetically fated for war (instinct) or does life create the competitive urge (frustration) which eventually outs in aggression? My own view is that there is no genetic endowment. A simple proof: if we had been genetically endowed with innate aggressive instincts, why would it be necessary for nations to work so hard to mold us into aggressive forms for war?

No, we can't blame aggression on our genes. The predominant scientific view is that man is typically *not* a killer. There is no innate impulse to kill. Arguments for the spontaneity of aggression just don't bear examination. The diversity of man's way of killing plus the rarity with which he uses these means proves conclusively that they are learned, not instinctive. The wretched Ik tribe in Africa are so worn down by life they will do anything. Except kill. The peaceful Tasaday and the Bushmen may save us by demonstrating that aggression was never instinctive. We have earned our terror.

Genes aside though, we all sort of sympathize with H. L. Mencken: "Every normal man must be tempted, at times, to spit on his hands, hoist the black flag, and begin slitting throats." And this societal stress causes men to revere war and its artifacts. Mishima, the famous Japanese writer, longed for a return of the samurai and when it didn't happen committed hara-kiri. Like S. A. Robinson's Miniver Cheevy, he ". . . missed the medieval grace of iron clothing."

The violence binge we're on now is partly the result of Vietnam. "Better a bad peace than a good war," the ancient wisdom reads. And Vietnam didn't qualify as a good war. Losing has left us with a frustrated yen to punch out, sort of the way the South has been since Lee packed it in at Appomattox. So the violence outs on the home front.

Nope, Vietnam wasn't a good war; it was a lousy war. It showed the truth of the Zen statement that you must be careful what you hate or you will become what you hate. We fought World War II motivated by self-defense, freedom, and other good values. But in hating the Nazis and the Japanese we came two decades later to take on their worst attributes. We visited a million or more deaths on peaceful Asians caught in ideological turmoil and gave even war a bad name.

But the worst part to me was that the techniques we used were so un-American. We have always been the good guys. We wear white hats, never shoot men in the backs, and love women, old folks, and kids. The Lone

Ranger always shot the crook with an antiseptic silver bullet through the wrist. But in Vietnam we took high and dreadful technology and used it viciously.* We spent over a million dollars with the most efficient and terrible ordnance known to history obliterating every peasant that faced us. We weren't fair.

And in the end we lost our butt. We lost because the guerrilla theory of the Viet Cong rested on a stronger base than our massive injections of men and material. The Viet Cong out-suffered and out-fought us. Their dead left little debris on the trails and battlefields beyond their bodies and occasionally some poetry; ours strewed cigarettes and condoms. The only solace is that we were wrong and lost. It could have been worse—we could have been right and lost. But, mind you, if we'd been right we wouldn't have lost.

After we lost, our President enjoined us that there should be no recriminations. Giant chutzpah, this, from a man who hawked the war safely from the sidelines. The ones who were right on the war suffered for years and many go on suffering. Those who were wrong now are in positions of power throughout our government and our social and economic life. They reap the fruits without being called to account. Moms Mabley's classic line: "Ain't nothing an old man can do for me but bring me a message from a young one," ain't bad. Old men are good at making war, but lousy at fighting it. If they had had to fight it, Vietnam wouldn't have happened.

Well, we finally extricated ourselves but even this was done with bad grace. Walter Goodman, in excoriating Kissinger on the silly Mayaguez caper in which we lost more men than we set out to rescue, wrote that the German, having lost his shirt in the pool hall (Vietnam), kicks the shoeshine boy (Cambodia) on the way out. That felicitous metaphor reminded me of a true story.

A big bird out of Chicago, affluent, goes into a pool hall downstate and starts shouldering the local yokels around. He tries to hustle them but is himself roped and hustled; one grizzled lank of a man in bib overalls runs 200 balls on him, upheavals him, sets down on him, and using the sole of Chicago's shoe, strikes a match and applies same to the hand-made Bull

---

*And it ended by taking us. Vietnam was no surgical operation. Civilians died out of all proportion to the combatants. The most indiscriminate antipersonnel weapon we used was the Cluster Bomb Unit (CBU). A CBU contains hundreds of bomblets, each slightly larger than a baseball, that will kill or wound any person in an area 300 by 900 meters. And each F4 could carry at least 15 of these babies. These things clearly violated international law and were the product of a military process which brooked no political input.

*The U.S.'s No-Win Grapple in Vietnam*

Durham cigarette he's been rolling all the while with the other hand.

"Stranger," says he, "You're sure high-strung, ain't ye?"

Well, Chicago leaves the place in high dudgeon and sees this slight black man, about 40, shining shoes just outside the door. There's nothing in it but frustrated Chicago just has to put his shoe through the shoeshine kit. The black man looks up slow and fast hitches up his belt. Chicago is all set to pulverize him when the first gent hollers from inside "Come on boys, teacher's got another city boy." Chicago didn't like the content of that yell and especially he didn't like the notion that the guy who had just manhandled him had called the black "teacher." He reasoned fast that what teacher taught might be graduate mayhem. So Chicago got out of there like a long-tailed cat leaving a room with ten rocking chairs in it—carefully but sincerely.

Our attitude towards violence was abysmal in the past. Regarding gladiatorial shows, W. E. H. Lecky wrote: "The mere desire for novelty impelled the people to every excess or refinement of barbarity. The simple combat became at last insipid, and every variety of atrocity was devised to stimulate the flagging interest. At one time a bear and a bull, chained together rolled in fierce contest along the sand; at another, criminals dressed in the skins of wild beasts were thrown to bulls, which were maddened by red-hot irons or by darts tipped with burning pitch. Four hundred bears were killed on a single day under Claudius. Under Nero, four hundred tigers fought with bulls and elephants; four hundred bears and three hundred lions were slaughtered by his soldiers. In a single day, at the dedication of the Colosseum by Titus, five thousand animals perished. Under Trajan, the games continued for one hundred and twenty-three successive days. Lions, tigers, elephants, rhinoceroses, hippopotami, giraffes, bulls, stags, even crocodiles and serpents, were employed to give novelty to the spectacle. Nor was any form of human suffering wanting. The first Gordian gave twelve spectacles, in each of which from one hundred and fifty to five hundred pair of gladiators appeared. Eight hundred pair fought at the triumph of Aurelian. Ten thousand men fought during the games of Trajan. Nero illuminated his gardens during the night by Christians burning in their pitchy shirts. Under Domitian, an army of feeble dwarfs was compelled to fight; and more than once, female gladiators descended to perish in the arena."

Some say we learned from Vietnam and that we are getting better in our attitudes toward violence. They are blind. We are only better at hiding the effect of our action from our consciences. We kill at a once-or-twice remove and thus can say: "It wasn't me." But of course it was. If anything we are far worse perpetrators of violence than our forebears because we are more efficient.

Just the other day, a friend told me that Italy during the Renaissance was full of violence and war but produced Michelangelo and Leonardo da Vinci while Switzerland has had 500 years of uninterrupted peace and it has produced the cuckoo clock. That lot of rot shows how hard it is to eradicate this devil in our blood and the excitement in our head. Competition is part of it. The effort expended in winning a game nowadays can be likened to that of a life-or-death struggle epochs ago. For the game today is merely sublimated warfare, ergo the effort to win at all costs.

*      *      *

I knew a street fighter in St. Louis in the early forties who had quite a string of successes. He couldn't abide defeat. It is reported that he even did what many claim is impossible—he beat Bad Sonny Liston in an alley in 18 minutes. My source is Larry Gains, the guy himself. He said he'd gotten the bear but he'd fought worse! Sonny, he said, was all shoulders and no root. Something to think about.

Anyhow Larry had one chink in his fighting armor—he loved children. Like Peter Pan, he never grew up. You put him with a couple kids and he'd be down on his knees serving as horsie. He loved it and would have agreed with Chesterton: "And I say that if a man had climbed to the stars / And found the secrets of the angels, / The best thing and the most useful thing he could do / Would be to come back and romp with children."

So once I asked Larry if it bothered him that a lot of the guys he'd put the quietus to had children. Wouldn't the kids cry to see dad hauling home a busted spleen or what have you?

I remember that his eyes widened and he sighed once slowly. He sat there for a full minute before mumbling that he'd never thought of it. No rationalizations about their old men deserving it, etcetera. Just that brief utterance. Then Larry walked out into the night, never to fight again.

A nice story. The truth of Taoism, Christianity, and all great religions is that the spirit of childhood can prevail over anything. For that's where the real action is. Let's get back there, folks!

# AN AFTERWORD

After my last book, *Western Boxing and World Wrestling*, I thought I was quit of the scribbling bit. I had said pretty much what I wanted to say, trying to illuminate the myriad varieties of world unarmed combat while cautioning against their commercialization. As information, I think my three books were useful but my caveats got flushed down the analytical drain. Hollywood and television, lying and cheating, have gone on beyond berserk.

Truly "when the going gets weird, the weird turn pro." Jimmy Cagney's "Public Enemy" raised social hackles against violence in 1932 by showing two killings. Now, a film without a hundred corpses couldn't make it a week before American audiences. Sylvester Stallone, who safely ensconced as a girls' chaperone in a posh Swiss school during the Vietnam War—while that other great warrior Dan Quayle quailed in the National Guard—later did in films what the U.S. couldn't do in reality: he beat the Vietnamese flat. On the unarmed side, it was no less lethal. Those icons of kung-fu and karate no-sweat non-contact, Bruce Lee and Chuck Norris, sort of danced and sort of acted (the acting, incredibly was even worse than the fake fighting), abetted by sound effects and camera shots and bodies toppled to the skies.

None of it was real, most of it was sociopathic, all of it was noxious mind pollution targeted on the median age of an unsteady, prepubescent 12 year-old. And when even this violence palled, eager movie moguls took the inoffensive turtle and ninjaed it into silly putty center stage. In the martial arts community even honest and capable teachers cut their consciences to these silly fashions or remained silent while the bogus bozos and gals revelled in it for the filthy lucre.

While at it, I want to respond to those who quarrel that my past work has been targeted on foreign masters and situations. They frequently ask: are there no American experts rivaling the great ones I've illuminated? Hollywood spews Rambo and Rocky and Bruce and Chuckie at us, but these birds are filmic creations irrelevant to real fighting. Marshall McLuhan, the late great sociologist, wrote that nothing happens in America unless it's been on television. So, just because the media hypes these as real doesn't make them real. Big bad Humphrey Bogart of the 30's and 40's locked himself in a toilet when a drunk little sailor kid got in his face one night at a party in Hollywood.

Most unarmed street fights are boring and brief with both warriors winded in five minutes, the only thing hurt being their hands from contacting the other's hard head. This reality would drive audiences away, leading the soulless Hollywood exploiters to lie, to spectacularize in order to make millions. The films are fixed dramatically—similar to pro wrestling—to deceive viewers. For me the only half-way redeeming film is "Remo Williams" because it is presented with humor—no one in it believes in what they are doing—as a classic leg-pull. All the others are dead serious about the meretriciousness and cheating (Chesterton says somewhere that the most decadent thing in the world is for a wrong to be done carefully), and thus are sociopathic, as bad for the viewer as dope.

When my publisher decided to reissue the paperback version of *Way of the Warrior*, he asked for a new chapter with which to garnish it. I was reluctant and stalled. But just at this time (Carl Jung called it synchronicity; Confucius, *Shr chung*—proper timing; and I, serendipity), I got a letter from my old partner in crime, R.W. Smith, from his retirement digs in the Carolina mountains. It stimulated me to go down and check out a real man and to revise somewhat my low opinion of American fighters. This man is by far the best master of combat I've encountered in America, beautifully caught by the Irish poet Joseph Campbell in his poem "A Fighting Man."

> A fighting-man he was,
> Guts and soul:
> A copper-skinned six-footer.
> Hewn out of the rock.
> Who would stand up against
> His hammer-lock?...
> Giants showed clean heels
> When his arm was bared.
> I've seen him swing an anvil
> Fifty feet.
> Break a bough in two,
> And tear a twisted sheet....

I can't improve on Bob's letter and interview, so I will simply move aside for him.

"John, I finally found a fellow down here who is of a calibre of your celebrated Pantheon. He's an Irish osteopath in his late 60's still going strong in an age of wimps. (It is surprising that at a time when TV is stuffed with ath-letes of all descriptions, there are few real men. This is because TV athletes are so specialized that if they move sideways an inch they are out of their ken.) But Tim Geoghegan has always been Olympian in his mastery. At one time he was wrestling and boxing champion and the strongest man in Ire-land. And Olympian in his durability. He's got a new-fangled weight machine and delights in having the weightlifting guys from the commercial gyms come round to stay with him on his routine.

"'They're pretty boys,' he says, 'with bulging deltoids and flaring lats—thanks to steroids—but they have no core, no depth, and they can't last twenty minutes. Back in the 50's when I was on the Pro wrestling circuit at Muscle Beach, California, a bunch of us wrestlers and genuine weight men would watch similar pret-ty boys do body balancing and weight tricks to lure the beach bunnies. Steroids weren't around then, but the guys were the same: they worked for definition (down deep, they were shallow, as someone observed about American politi-cians recently) rather than for real strength and health. One of our number, Ivan Kameroff, a good big wrestler and lifter, while smoking a cigar, would challenge the guys to press their bodyweight overhead. Most couldn't, but then they'd dare big Ivan to do it. He'd light his cigar and load the bar to 300 pounds. Then, smiling broadly and puff-ing his stogie, he would press it ten (!) times overhead. The boys vanished leaving the girls to the men.'

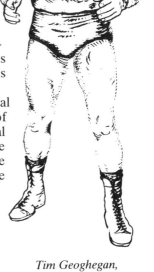

"Dr. Tim Geoghegan regards most martial arts he's seen in America with a mixture of amusement and dudgeon. Appearing at several combatives workshops he was shocked by the low fighting level and high arrogance of the stars. They were impressed by his "combative wrestling" but not hip enough really to see its value. In Atlanta, he invited the top karateka to take a free chop at his throat. Despite the man's wife begging Tim to reconsider—her husband's chop could kill, she cautioned—Tim smiled and said he'd risk it. Hubby hauled back and took his swipe at Tim's caro-

*Tim Geoghegan,*
*a fighter in a world of wimps*

tid artery (which can cause a heart reflex and death—so readers should not try this). Tim continued smiling but observed that it wasn't very strong.

"Then in a workshop in North Carolina, an expert in Filipino arts, a student of Bruce Lee, told Tim he could escape his takedown. Tim started and the guy tried to turn out—Tim scoffed later, 'Hell, he was only 135 pounds—and counter, but was flattened for his pains.' Tim was asked what the guy said then.

"'Well, he said nothing. When he turned he went the wrong way—actually, either way would've been the wrong way—and I put a headlock-sleeper on him and he was out before he hit the floor. Previously the chap had invited me to teach a seminar in California, but I never heard from him again.'

"And he never will. California has a relationship to real martial arts like Dracula had to garlic. Here's how our interview went:

(S) Nineteen years after being born in Leitrim County, Ireland, in 1922, you won the title of the strongest man in the country. How did you do it?

(G) I came from a family of athletes. My father could box with the best of them and could jump up and touch both feet at the level of his forehead besides being powerful at lifting. In fact, we lost him at 33 when he tried to lift his car back onto an icy road (I believe the same sort of thing happened to strongman Eugene Sandow). I had the genes, good food to meet my appetite, and enormous energy. At 19, a mere stripling but bulking out near 200 pounds, I defeated Ireland's top strongman, John Moriarity, him with thirty years on me. Then I joined the John Duffy Circus as "Young Atlas" and really got indoctrinated in the strength game. I lifted all kinds of weights, took on all comers in boxing and wrestling, and used my young energy to the fullest.

If someone challenged me to lift a horse, I lifted a horse (though I didn't take the time to copy my friend Paul Baillergeon, who carried a full-grown 1,300 pound horse up a tree!). I successfully resisted the power of two giant Clydesdales pulling in opposite directions. I was stimulated by challenge. With my teeth, I pulled a double-decker bus full of people and swung (a 6 foot chain attached to his belt) a 240-pound man around my body. I could rip a deck of new cards bought in a store by a neutral party in half without opening the box and in quarters out of the box. Big city phone directories were a breeze, and in top form I could tear them from the closed, glued side. I've had two men stand on a 2 by 4 across my neck and even had a truck run up it without effect, but I never achieved Farmer Burns' feat of actually hanging himself. Burns was a great wrestler: figuring the bodyweight, even better than his best student, Frank Gotch. After his competitive days were over, Burns, who had developed his neck muscles to an extraordinary degree, would let himself be dropped from a height with a noose around his neck and hang twenty minutes without injury. There were real necks in those days!

(S) Did you ever invent a stunt that no one else could do?

(G) One I did in the circus might fit that category. I'd take 56-pound weights, one in each hand, and climb up on three chairs, jumping over the back of the third chair, onto a see-saw with a 140-pound bar at the other end. When my bodyweight hit the board I'd let go of the dumbbells and catch the barbell that had been shot up from the other end of the board on my neck. Ah, those were the days!

(S) How did your circus career end?

(G) In near disaster. I understand that the Chinese character for "crisis" has two components: one translates "danger," the other, "opportunity." That's how it was then. Once in Belfast I was on my back supporting a platform up which a rider rode on a horse. Then I would leg press both rider and horse several times. For some reason—it was probably accidental but the rider did fancy the same girl I did—he didn't stop and rode the horse over the side, forcing it to jump. This abrupt shift in weight profoundly displaced my fifth lumbar vertebrae and sacrum.

Though I was dragging my left leg and could only do certain routines, I managed to get through the last week of the engagement. Then I went to Dublin where the doctors gave me the bad news that I would need a body cast for six months and then crutches the rest of my life. In great pain and some despair I took the advice of a friend and went to a retired osteopath, Dr. D. Byrne, who learned his trade while serving in India as a high court judge for the British administration. My friend and Dr. Byrne strapped me to a table, stabilized my sacrum, and pulled like hell (this was done without anesthesia which I couldn't abide). There was a sound like a millstone turning as the fifth lumbar rotated on the sacrum to its normal position. In about a minute I had been made whole by a man who knew how to maintain and correct the body. As I arose I asked him what I owed him and he said "Your life." This incident, then, had danger and opportunity. When I was made whole I resolved to spend my life in osteopathy helping others as Dr. Byrne had helped me. I must add that Dr. Byrne was also the man who introduced me to the study of yoga, which I practiced in the West and in India and Pakistan. My formal osteopathic training, though, was done under Dr. F. Taylor, one of the best in England and the man who took what Dr. Byrne had restored and made into the healer I now am.

(S) Please dilate on your boxing career.

(G) Sure. To make a long story interesting, as the saying goes, I got started in what we called "crossroads boxing" of the bare-fisted variety by being born into a fighting family. My father was an extraordinary athlete. His brothers and sons would periodically mix it up with others at obscure cross- roads, and when he died I succeeded him. I would meet challenges Sundays after church and over the years had perhaps thirty to forty of them. The fights were hard-boned things but if you knocked a man down there was no kicking or piling on. You helped him up and had a meal somewhere with him. We were gentlemen. Only in England or America was there the ani- mosity that carried over into kicking and other dirty tactics.

A bit later in the John Duffy circus I had well over 100 bouts against all comers, sort of like booth boxing. We used gloves and it wasn't long before I was being handled by excellent British trainers. The upshot was that I was approached by the head of the board controlling Irish amateur boxing in company with Jack Solomon, head of British pro boxing, who tried to talk me into facing Bruce Woodcock and Freddy Mills after "bringing me along easy." But I begged off. I didn't like the blood-and-gore style of British box- ing—copying the American—and I didn't want my brains scrambled for the kind of money they were willing to pay. And by then I was doing well at wrestling and thinking of trying my luck in America. I've never regretted my decision.

(S) Did you have a philosophy in boxing?

(G) My father told me that the first thing you do is respect your oppo- nent. You don't look at him and say "This guy is easy." Starting out, I'd throw a few straight lefts to stretch him out. Stretching was one of my favorite tactics because you could finish a match quite quickly with a straight left which might not even damage, but just push him straight back. And when his head was straight back, I would solar-plex him. I discovered that very early by reading how Bob Fitzsimmons at 185 pounds had stretched James Corbett at 215 pounds and solar-plexed him. I thought about that and developed it over a period of years. It worked well in the circus when I had to take on all comers. The toughest of these were soldiers, many of whom had fought in cities and knew ringcraft. But most were local toughs who terrorized towns and, with booze in them, wanted to show the home folks that they could whip outsiders too. They were easy to handle: out they'd charge wildly swinging and two swift punches would end it.

It helped if you could hit hard and the Geoghegan brothers' hard hit- ting was natural. If Jimmy Wilde (100 pounds) could prevail in boxing booths against all weights, it was much easier for me at 200 pounds to handle the local bruisers. But when you met someone with talent you had to feel him out, respecting him, and feint him into revealing his skill. I like to counter, get him to miss a couple of times. Patience is a real virtue inside and outside the ring. When even a steady fighter misses with both hands a few times it unhinges him a bit and he starts to think "Good God, I can't hit this man. What's happening?" That kind of analysis, brief as it is, in a reflexive affair like boxing creates a vacancy in his mind, and that's when I'd counter.

(S) In "reading" your opponent what did you cue on?

(G) The eyes, I watched his eyes—they don't lie. In jabbing I'd measure him, never expending too much energy. But I wouldn't let him know that I could punch any harder until an opening came through my feint or his force. Only then would I use much strength. There's an old saying, "Beware the power of a patient man."

(S) Generally then, you would fight a more defensive style than we see in America these days?

(G) Quite right. I was nurtured in the British style which early this century was characterized by a flair for the defensive. Indeed, in scoring matches, British judges gave a defensive duck or slip twice the credit that they did an offensive jab or a cross. So it was genteel, geared more to a points decision than a knockout. Pedlar Palmer was a master at this kind of boxing. But some could punch as well as box. Little Jimmy Wilde, weighing in at 100 pounds, could beat good boxers who out-weighed him 50 pounds. And in boxing booths where he stood off all comers he'd tire the local 200-pound bullies and then blast them out with his tiny, power-laden fists. Later in life, Wilde got into refereeing wrestling matches and I came to know him quite well. Pound-for-pound he has to rank as one of the truly superior battlers in the modern era. He proved that you didn't have to be big to be a knockout artist. Once he told me that the prime thing was speed: a plowhorse, he said, could kick you in the chest and put you in the next field, but when a racehorse kicks you he breaks your chest!

(S) How did you get started wrestling?

(G) In Ireland there was big Pat Gibbons, 330 pounds in his stocking feet. And I went to his gym to try the grappling game. He pinned me and I was a zoo trying to get free. But couldn't. He was proud of his prowess, but he forgot that I was a raw novice. In six weeks I reversed the roles and Pat couldn't peel my 210 pounds off. Then in the north of England I got some expert training in the Lancashire and other styles of wrestling and joined the pro circuit.

In the old days, before the big wrestling combines began, the giants in America were Farmer Burns and Frank Gotch out of Iowa. Burns was a mentor to Gotch, John Pesek, Fred Grubmier, and many other fine wrestlers. And, of course, you had the great George Hackenschmidt and other Europeans.

These were shooters, not show-men. They had will—a very important trait. They were far superior to boxers and needed no trainers. Unlike boxers, they wrestled every day in training and in matches and kept themselves fit. Nowadays, you have world boxing champs with twenty fights, which would be unheard of in wrestling. Gama, the great Indian wrestler, came to Europe and demolished everyone. The second best in the world at the time was his brother, also undefeated. In jacketed wrestling, the Japanese judoka were supreme, S. Yokoyama and that crew. They used throws, pins, and locks—the whole shebang.

In England in Lancashire and other northern places they practiced a unique wrestling which featured locks and other techniques illegal elsewhere. This is the form of wrestling I was nurtured on in Ireland and England. Not sportive so much as combatively dangerous.

One of the greatest American shooters was Fred Grubmier. He didn't like the wrestling trusts but had his own way of making money. He'd go into a town in the 1940's, a gangly guy in overalls. He'd bet $10 that he could beat anyone in town in pool and when he lost he'd admit he was a better footracer and would bet $50 against the town. Again he'd be beaten. Next, were there any boxers about? He had $100 that said he could whip the best around. Again, he lost. By this time the town felt sorry for the simple fellow, but when he allowed as how he was a better grappler than boxer and would back it up with his last $1000 the town flushed pity down the drain and went out and brought in a guy who'd once given the great John Pesek trouble. The match started and, miraculously, after being bashed around the ring and nearly pinned a half dozen times, the stranger seemed to get better in a flash, the local was nailed to the mat, and Grubmier with his swag was off to similar hustling in distant towns.

In time, the combines took over in America and shooting gave way to show. Jim Londos (210 pounds) was a great showman but couldn't handle the big boys like Strangler Lewis (250 pounds). Lewis was so strong that good ground wrestlers couldn't best him because they couldn't get behind him or couldn't take him down. Dick Shikat and Hans Steinke were superior to Lewis only on the ground.

The days of shooters like Hackenschmidt, Gotch, and Pesek are long gone. Jack Sherry came along later but refused to show. Lou Thesz and Bert Assirati were good shooters who were forced to show to make a living. Thesz was a great wrestler, one of the best since the 40's. His father had been champion in Hungary where free-style predominated. He was skilled and very strong. Late in his career I had three matches with him. Two were draws and in the third I had a sleeper on him and he drop-kicked me out of the ring. Though he then passed out and was unconscious, he was declared the winner when I couldn't get back into the ring within the ten count.

Assirati, the European champion in the 30's and 40's, was in Thesz's class and was a truly unique athlete. After beating the best in Europe, Bert came to America in 1933 and wrestled 65 times, winning 63—besting Joe Stecher, Ray Steele, W. Zbyszko, and other top dogs, and drawing twice, with Steele and the formidable Hans Steinke. I wrestled him three or four times, all draws, when he was past his prime. His top weight was 270 pounds on a short frame. But what power! He could dead-lift 800 pounds and do a one-leg squat shouldering 200 pounds which was equivalent to squatting with 645 pounds on both legs! Once he squatted continuously for a half-hour with a 235-pound barbell on his shoulders. For fun, he would load up with two heavy dumbbells and jump on a chair 100 times. Besides such strength routines, he was a prodigious gymnast capable of a one-hand stand, a back flip, a crucifix on the rings, and one of two best of all time at the one-arm chin—doing three repetitions!

Strangler Lewis managed me for two years (1949-50) and I learned much from him though he was an old man by then. He made too much money from me and I broke away after two years. But I benefited because he got me into Canada. At that time the Canadian heavies bulked out at 250 pounds and above, while I was only 210 pounds. Lewis liked me because of my sleeper which made weight irrelevant. It brought them all down to size. I didn't learn my sleeper from Lewis but developed it from a choke against both carotids taught me in London during World War II by Dr. Higami Kasutu, a ju-jitsu adept in his 80's. I blended it with a one-carotid choke I got from Indian wrestling. It was so decisive that I would sometimes have the ring full of the bodies of challengers from the audience. In Toronto once I had twenty asleep at the same time.

When Harold ("Oddjob") Sakata of "James Bond" movie fame first met me in California he couldn't believe that I could choke him out and, when he came to, thought he was back in Montreal a week before, and that his opponent there had put him out. I dropped a fellow in Halifax, Nova Scotia, and, as he was coming around, I asked him how it felt. "I tried to struggle even though it didn't feel like you were choking me," he said, "but then everything went blank." He writhed and talked and actually thought he was in bed with Marilyn Monroe and I had to take the microphone away from him lest he describe the orgasm.

Back in England, in Cheltenham, a bully who was a 260-pound bouncer at the largest nightclub, came forward sneering at the sleeper. I said, "It's simple enough," spun him around and put him down and out. I brought him out of it and, wild-eyed, he threw a roundhouse at me. I ducked and spun him and dropped him again. As I resuscitated him, I asked, "Hey, are you gonna be a good boy?" and he meekly answered, "Yes sir" to the delight of the fans.

But the sleeper was only a part of my skill. When I first came to America, the pro wrestling tycoon Paul Bowser sent Wilbur Nead (AAU national heavyweight champ in 1940) to test me at the Boston YMCA. Nead tried everything he knew to take me off my feet but failed. Every time he leg-dived me I'd face-lock him and twist his neck into a dangerous position. Frustrated, he said, "You know, you're doing something that no one has ever done before." I told him maybe not in America, but in Europe that was a routine response to a leg-dive. He was a helluva leg wrestler and we became good friends.

Out in Los Angeles, I ran into an ex-shooter, Hugh Nichols, who was promoting TV wrestling. Hearing I was a former strongman he was quickly sceptical. "You're an Irish strongman and I'm a hard-boiled American. Let me prove it." He got a new deck of cards and told me to tear them in two. I did better—I tore them in quarters. It made him a believer. He was around 65 then (1949) and when Wayne Martin (three time NCAA champion, 1934-36; voted outstanding college wrestler in 1936) berated Rick Barry and Danny McShane, top TV wrestlers, Nichols braced him.

"You wrestle?"

"Yeah, I was national collegiate champion."

"Well," said Nichols, "I'm 65 and haven't wrestled for twenty years, you look about 30. Would you like to try a fall?"

"Old man, I'd kill you," rejoined Martin, "you'd have a heart attack."

Nichols dropped onto his side and as the cocky Martin reached for him he double wristlocked him and trapped him with his leg. Martin yelped to Nichols to let him up, got up, and told him he couldn't do it again. By this time Nichols was also up and Martin leg-dived him. Nichols face-locked him into a double wristlock and trapped his leg again. And said, "Kid, when you learn to wrestle come and see me again."

So you see, there were some good grapplers involved in the pro wrestling trade. And not just in the promotion end, but some were like me—trying to earn a living while studying for a career.

(S) Former All-American footballer Herman Hickman went on the pro wrestling circuit in the 30's. They had a code in which he was "Cannonball" and George Zaharias (who married the female athlete, Babe Didrickson) was "Subway" (so-called because the first time he visited New York City he got lost in the subway). Instructions on upcoming matches would go out by Western Union and be confirmed on the rival Postal Tele-graph. A typical wire might read: "Cannonball moon Subway around 35 confirm" which simply meant that Hickman would lose to Zaharias (look up at the moon) in 35 minutes. In talking about those times, Hickman tried to reject the idea that wrestling was rehearsed by saying something to the effect that wrestlers must have a feel for the crowd and build to the proper dramatic climax. Did your circuit operate along the lines Hickman suggests and how do you like his notion that the bouts aren't fixed?

(G) Logistically, we operated similarly. But his attempt to say the bouts weren't fixed is nonsense. Is a broadway show rehearsed? If the result is known—and it is—then the script can be massaged any number of ways, but it is still rehearsed. Sure, against a good wrestler I always semi-shot regardless of prior arrangements about the result. There was pride in avoid-ing being trapped by a sharp shooter. But the result was fixed by business considerations and was immutable. For me, it simply was a way to use the skills I had to support the education I needed to become a doctor. But this never blinded me to the fact that it was show, not even as competitive as my strength routines in the circus. Murray Kempton, one of America's finest writers, saw it steadily and whole when he said that the major defect in pro wrestling was its absence of honest passion.

(S) What was your funniest moment in the ring?

(G) In 1964 or 1965 I went into a televised tag-team bout in Vancouver, B.C., against a Texan who, like most Texans, carried around the enormous weight of his ego: he thought of himself as super-tough, a legend in his own mind. Right off he elbowed me on the chin. Even though I was surprised, my reflexes saved me and I was only stunned. But enough so that I forgot cir-cumstances and, as we closed, I hit him square with my elbow. As he col-lapsed I realized, with horror, that we were slated to wrestle for five more minutes until commercials came on. I face-locked him and rolled his uncon-scious form around the ring. Just before the time expired and I flopped him toward where his tagging partner stood, he began to show a little life. It was one of the strangest bouts I was ever in.

(S) How about outside the ring?

(G) Oh, there were many hilarious moments with the lads, and seri-ous ones with promoters trying to short-change us. When Lewis was man-aging me, I remember an Aussie amateur coming over to learn to wrestle. He wanted to know what to eat to gain strength. One of the boys told him to try dog biscuits: "They make your jaws strong." So the poor guy subsisted on dog biscuits for a week before one of the wives had pity on him and let him in on the joke. There was always a lot of ribbing. You'd get a new guy to get down on all fours then say "Now lift one of your hind legs" and, when he did, you'd say, "Good doggy."

(S) But you were well read and pretty sensitive and the circuit must have been bleak and full of ennui. How did you cope with it when you weren't in the ring?

(G) Easy. When I traveled around by train to the wrestling venues I always took my medical books with me and studied. When I was off, I'd seek out a library and spend much time there. I lived in libraries. I remember especially the library at the University of London where I spent hundreds of hours pursuing leads my teachers gave me. I'd go in at 11 a.m. and sometimes forget to eat and rush out to wrestle at 9 p.m. with an empty stomach. When I was young I took the lasses to dances but, once, my motorcycle gave out and after pushing the blasted thing uphill for twenty miles, dancing receded and athletics won out.

Combining books and athletics got me degrees and certificates in osteopathy, physiotherapy, hypnotherapy, psychology, Hatha and Raja yoga, and jujutsu, among other disciplines. I searched for knowledge and achieved a bit, though whether it has mellowed and evolved into wisdom is not for me to say.

(S) What was the big problem in wrestling?

(G) For old-timers it was trachoma. The mats after a while were a vile brew of sputum, resin, and blood, and this bred trachoma which could and did blind some wrestlers. The earlier treatment, copper sulfate, which the afflicted would rub into the eyes to kill the microscopic germ, was harsh therapy. Nowadays, antibiotics clear it up in short order and, of course mats are more hygienic.

But the big problem in my time was accidents. As I rolled out of a ring in Houston once during this period, a dirty nail stuck in my kneecap. I put some alcohol on it but by the next night in Louisiana it was swollen and I had to beat my man from a standing position. Luckily, he wasn't much and I won without difficulty. The Houston doctors told me the kneecap was so infected they'd have to cut it off. I didn't like the sound of that and went to an old osteopath friend, Dr. Connors in Dallas, and he prescribed a regime of soaking in red-hot towels while drinking orange juice and ingesting potassium. When the knee normalized, he drained the infection and ordered me to bed for six weeks. It worked and I was able to continue wrestling.

(S) How do you regard pro wrestling these days?

(G) TV wrestling today is a degraded thing done by loud, berserk people, most of them pumped up by hormones, almost none of whom can wrestle. It is an unseemly business, so bad is is not even funny enough to be farce. The fact that it commands large audiences says some profound things about the yahoos abroad in this benighted land. Really good shooters, if bucks are more important than their honor, only participate if they are willing to do business.

(S) The Asians lay great stress on not "spending" one's sperm promiscuously. Our "media" athletes deride this notion. What do you think?

(G) I agree with the Asians. When young, I read an Irish writer who said that a drop of sperm equated to an ounce of blood, thus was too precious to be wasted. It is a tremendous force readily seen in nature. It takes two or three men to restrain a stallion before he procreates. After being with a mare the same horse can be easily held down. Most Americans may believe that sexuality has nothing to do with boxing or competitive wrestling, but most fighters I knew and trained with would save their essence for thirty days before a fight in order to be at their peak of power.

(S) You've devoted much of your life to helping people help themselves through their bodies. Just now drugs seem to be sucking the virility from the so-called civilized world.

(G) There are two things in the world, God and inertia. In the present era we seem to have put God on hold, leaving the field to inertia. We don't have the will to put forth the effort to cope with problems. Consumerists all, we want a magic pill. And the big secret in life is that there isn't one. People who take drugs, including alcohol and cigarettes, do so because they're trying to free themselves from their body, trying to escape. The West considers the body gross, something to be transcended. I spent much time in India and Pakistan studying yoga, and there the body was regarded almost as sacred, not something to escape from. A smoker simply lacks the gumption to say "no" to a vile habit. Educators and psychiatrists help us to face life, but, essentially, we must fight the fight ourselves. Our bodies, even when wounded, can help our brains provide positive reinforcement. To be positive in your outlook, to say I can do this or that is the beginning of everything. All that I've ever accomplished I had to first believe I could do.

Let me give you an example. Doug Hepburn, former world weightlifting champion was a good friend of mine. His father, a top Canadian journalist, was dogged all his days by alcoholism and died destitute. Doug developed polio in his left leg at six. The leg was so thin that even after years of training, all you could see were the bones and tendons where the calf was supposed to be, a limb only half the thickness of a normal man's and a quarter of the thickness of his right leg. And yet, disguising the tiny leg with six pairs of heavy socks, he became the strongest man in the world. Put 400 pounds on his shoulders and he'd press it. Remembering the waste of his brilliant father, he conceived a positive image that became pure power. He told me that as he worked alone he concentrated on his shadow thrown on the wall by the light behind him. Standing over the bar he would psych himself up and actually project onto his shadow the things that he wanted to be and do. The shadow became the shadow of him psyching himself up. He'd look at it and mentally project from that shadow his arms overhead with the barbell high. He didn't know until years later when I told him of the Indian strongmen's "shadow technique" that the Indians did the same thing he'd come to do intuitively. It is an imaging method, sure, but it must be positive. Insane asylums are filled with folk degraded by wrong imaging. So one must be careful: when you are wronged in life, take a lesson from Doug Hepburn—don't judge the person too harshly lest you hurt yourself. Think positively!

This kind of thinking got me involved in hypnotherapy. Introduced to it by Dr. Maurice Nicoll who wrote the seminal work on Gurdjieff, I studied it for five years in Bloomsbury. I continued my lessons by mail after I came to America and returned to England in 1953 and 1963 where Nicoll supervised further research leading to certification as a hypnotherapist. The normal mind is similar to sleepwalking when compared to the higher mind achieved through hypnosis. In London we produced a blister on a subject's arm by merely suggesting that a pencil we rubbed on it was a cigarette lighter. By hypnosis nine-tenths of our mind that is never used is opened up. It is not sleep—it is a new route to the subconscious.

(S) But it can be exploitative when used in advertising.

(G) Certainly. The evidence is everywhere. America is a nation of consumers avid to believe any shill and buy any product. Advertisers know that psychology is king and that politics and economics are sectors of it, not the other way round. Take our teens—they are manipulated coming and going. Try to listen to their egregious music: without lyrics and melody it can't be sung, hummed, or whistled. The kids were motivated into buying this two-beat cacophony by being told it would make them free. And all the while they helped the advertiser enslave them. They are now spoiled, incoherent, lazy, and frightened. Kahlil Gibran, the Lebanese poet, caught them in his line, "Is not the dread of thirst when your well is full, thirst that is unquenchable?"

(S) What's the solution?

(G) The quickest is to burn all TV sets, but advertisers wouldn't permit that so I'd change the educational system and mandate a lot of directed physical exercise in the schools that would put the children back in their bodies. Few of them are even aware of their bodies, thus are vulnerable to the collective consumerist pitches made to them. When they lose contact with their bodies, their mental and physical health suffers. Getting their bodies back will make them individuals again, persons able to resist the lies of the advertisers. Yoga, taichi, wrestling, and judo are a few of the old, time-honored disciplines that could help children back on the right track. Remember: our civilization depends on these children!

*     *     *

So there you have it: a real warrior in America. A strong man who scoffs at steroids and filmic clowns like Arnold and Sylvester—even their names conjure up pussycats rather than fighters—and laughs at the show rassling and much of the bilge passing for boxing these days. But above all, a quiet man with a voice softer even than Dempsey's or Marciano's, a gentle man able "to connect the tender and tough," in Rilke's fine phrase.

In our present manic phase we don't deserve him, but God bless us all, let's cherish him.